The Second World War on the Eastern Front

The Second World War on the Eastern Front

Lee Baker

Harlow, England • London • New York • Boston • San Francisco • Toronto
Sydney • Tokyo • Singapore • Hong Kong • Seoul • Taipei • New Delhi
Cape Town • Madrid • Mexico City • Amsterdam • Munich • Paris • Milan

PEARSON EDUCATION LIMITED

Edinburgh Gate
Harlow CM20 2JE
United Kingdom
Tel: +44 (0)1279 623623
Fax: +44 (0)1279 431059
Website: www.pearsoned.co.uk

First edition published in Great Britain in 2009

ISBN: 978-1-4058-4063-7

British Library Cataloguing in Publication Data
A CIP catalogue record for this book can be obtained from the British Library

Library of Congress Cataloging in Publication Data
Baker, Lee, 1961–
    The Second World War on the Eastern Front / Lee Baker. – 1st ed.
       p. cm.
    Includes bibliographical references and index.
    ISBN 978-1-4058-4063-7 (pbk.)
    1. World War, 1939–1945–Campaigns–Eastern Front.   2. World War, 1939–1945–
Europe, Eastern.   3. World War, 1939–1945–Soviet Union.   4. World War, 1939–145–
Campaigns–Eastern Front–Sources.   5. World War, 1939–1945–Europe, Eastern–Sources.
6. World War, 1939–1945–Soviet Union–Sources.   I. Title.
    D764.B24355 2009
    940.54′217–dc22

                                                                          2009011687

10   9   8   7   6   5   4   3   2   1
13   12   11   10   09

Set by 35 in 10/13.5pt Berkeley Book
Printed and bound in Malaysia (CTP-VVP)

The Publisher's policy is to use paper manufactured from sustainable forests.

Introduction to the Series

History is a narrative constructed by historians from traces left by the past. Historical enquiry is often driven by contemporary issues and, in consequence, historical narratives are constantly reconsidered, reconstructed and reshaped. The fact that different historians have different perspectives on issues means that there is also often controversy and no universally agreed version of past events. *Seminar Studies in History* was designed to bridge the gap between current research and debate, and the broad, popular general surveys that often date rapidly.

The volumes in the series are written by historians who are not only familiar with the latest research and current debates concerning their topic, but who have themselves contributed to our understanding of the subject. The books are intended to provide the reader with a clear introduction to a major topic in history. They provide both a narrative of events and a critical analysis of contemporary interpretations. They include the kinds of tools generally omitted from specialist monographs: a chronology of events, a glossary of terms and brief biographies of 'who's who'. They also include bibliographical essays in order to guide students to the literature on various aspects of the subject. Students and teachers alike will find that the selection of documents will stimulate discussion and offer insight into the raw materials used by historians in their attempt to understand the past.

Clive Emsley and Gordon Martel
Series Editors

I thank my wife, Pamela, for her continued support in every endeavor, whether professional or personal, and Tuula and Elizabeth for all their help.

Contents

Acknowledgements

We are grateful to the following for permission to reproduce copyright material:

Document 1 from *Nazism: a History in Documents and Eyewitness Accounts, 1919–1945*, vol. 2, New York: Schocken Books (Noakes, J., and G. Pridham, 1988), pp. 743–4; Document 2 from *Nazi-Soviet Relations 1939–1941: Documents from the Archives of the German Foreign Office*, Washington, DC., USGPO (United States Department of State, 1948), pp. 349–53; Document 3 from *Hitler's War Directives, 1939–1945* (London: Sidgwick and Jackson, 1964), pp. 49–51 (Trevor-Roper, H.R., ed.) (© 1964 H.R. Trevor-Roper), reproduced by permission of PFD (www.pfd.co.uk) on behalf of The Literary Estate of Sir H.R. Trevor-Roper; Document 4 from *Nazi Conspiracy and Aggression* vol. III, Washington, DC., USGPO (Office of the US Chief of Counsel for Prosecution of Axis Criminality, 1946), p. 447; Document 5 from *Nazi Conspiracy and Aggression* vol. III, Washington, DC., USGPO (Office of the US Chief of Counsel for Prosecution of Axis Criminality, 1946), pp. 637–8; Document 7 adapted from *The Great Patriotic War of the Soviet Union*, New York: International Publishers (Stalin, J., 1945), pp. 9–17, permission from International Publishers Co/New York; Document 8 from *Nazi Conspiracy and Aggression* vol. VI, Washington, DC., USGPO (Office of the US Chief of Counsel for Prosecution of Axis Criminality, 1946), p. 876; Document 9 from *The Halder War Diary, 1939–1942*, Novato, CA: Presidio (Halder, F., edited by Charles Burdick and Hans-Adolf Jacobsen, 1988), pp. 446–7 (© 1988 by Charles Burdick). Used by permission of Presidio Press, an imprint of The Ballantine Publishing Group, a division of Random House, Inc.; Document 10 from *The Halder War Diary, 1939–1942*, Novato, CA: Presidio (Halder, F., edited by Charles Burdick and Hans-Adolf Jacobsen, 1988), p. 506 (© 1988 by Charles Burdick). Used by permission of Presidio Press, an imprint of The Ballantine Publishing Group, a division of Random House, Inc.; Document 11 from *Nazi Conspiracy and Aggression*,

VIII, Washington, DC., USGPO (Office of the US Chief for Prosecution of Axis Criminality, 1946), pp. 585–7; Document 12 from *Hitler's Table Talk, 1941–1944: His Private Conversations*, New York: Enigma Books (Trevor-Roper, H., ed., 1953), p. 94, *Hitler's Table Talk 1941–1944: His Private Conversations* by Francois Genoud, edited by Hugh Trevor-Roper. Published by Weidenfeld and Nicolson, an imprint of the Orion Publishing Group, London; Document 13 from *Hitler's War Directives, 1939–1945* (London: Sidgwick and Jackson, 1964), pp. 106–7, (Trevor-Roper, H.R., ed.) (© 1964 H.R. Trevor-Roper) reproduced by permission of PFD (www.pfd.co.uk) on behalf of The Literary Estate of Sir H.R. Trevor-Roper; Document 14 from *Hitler's Table Talk, 1941–1944*, New York: Enigma Books (Trevor-Roper, H., 1939), pp. 200–1, 220, *Hitler's Table Talk 1941–1944: His Private Conversations* by Francois Genoud, edited by Hugh Trevor-Roper. Published by Weidenfeld and Nicolson, an imprint of the Orion Publishing Group, London; Document 15 from *Hitler's War Directives, 1939–1945* (London: Sidgwick and Jackson, 1964), pp.116–17 (Trevor-Roper, H.R., ed.) (© 1964 H.R. Trevor-Roper) reproduced by permission of PFD (www.pfd.co.uk) on behalf of The Literary Estate of Sir H.R. Trevor-Roper; Document 16 from *Companion to Colossus Reborn: Key Documents and Statistics*, Lawrence: University Press of Kansas (Glantz, D.M., 2005), pp. 17–21; Document 17 from *Nazi Conspiracy and Aggression*, VIII, Washington, DC., USGPO (Office of the US Chief for Prosecution of Axis Criminality, 1946), pp. 696–8; Document 19 from *Hitler's War Directives, 1939–1945* (London: Sidgwick and Jackson, 1964), pp. 159–60 (Trevor-Roper, H.R., ed.) (© 1964 H.R. Trevor-Roper) reproduced by permission of PFD (www.pfd.co.uk) on behalf of The Literary Estate of Sir H.R. Trevor-Roper; Document 20 from *800 Days on the Eastern Front*, Lawrence: University Press of Kansas (Litvin, N.; translated and edited by Stuart Britton, 2007), p. 69; Document 21 from *Adventures in My Youth: A German Soldier on the Eastern Front, 1941–45*, Solihull: Helion & Company (Scheiderbauer, A., 2003), pp. 133–4; Document 23 from H.R. Trevor-Roper, ed., *Hitler's War Directives, 1939–1945* (London: Sidgwick and Jackson, 1964), pp. 212–13 (© 1964 H.R. Trevor-Roper) reproduced by permission of PFD (www.pfd.co.uk) on behalf of The Literary Estate of Sir H.R. Trevor-Roper.

We are grateful to the following for permission to reproduce photographs:

Plate 1 Hulton Archive/Staff; Plate 2 United States Holocaust Memorial Museum: Jerzy Tomaszewski; Plate 3 Imagno/Contributor; Plate 4 Keystone/Stringer; Plate 5 Time Life Pictures/Stringer; Plate 6 Mansell/Stringer; Plates

7, 8 Keystone/Stringer; Plate 9 G. Lipskerov/Contributor; Plate 10 Victor
Temin/Contributor.

In some instances we have been unable to trace the owners of copyright
material, and we would appreciate any information that would enable us to
do so.

List of Maps

List of Plates

Chronology

1939

23 August German–Soviet Pact signed.

1 September Germany invades Poland, the Second World War begins 3 September.

17 September The USSR invades Poland.

1940

22 June France agrees to an armistice with Germany.

21 July Hitler orders plans for an invasion of the USSR.

31 July Second meeting at which Hitler makes clear his intention to attack the USSR.

4 August Marcks plan presented to OKW.

6 December OKW ordered to formulate a plan for an invasion.

18 December Directive for 'Operation Barbarossa' issued.

1941

26 March Agreement between *SS* and the Army regarding *Einsatzgruppen*.

19 May Order regarding German troop behavior during the campaign.

6 June 'Commissar Order' issued.

22 June The German armed forces launch 'Operation Barbarossa' at 3:15 am.

23 June Soviets create *Stavka*.

28 June Germans capture Minsk.

3 July Stalin's speech to the Soviet people.

7 July The Jews of Minsk are registered and forced to move into a ghetto.

16 July Germans capture Smolensk.

19 July Sixth Army orders that Jews will be shot in reprisal for partisan attacks when the perpetrators cannot be located.

25 July	Mass murder of Jews in the Zhitomir region begins.
20 August	Siege of Leningrad begins.
21 August	90 Jewish children burned alive on Reichenau's orders.
19 September	Germans capture Kiev; 5000 Jews murdered in Vinnitsa and another 15 000 in Berdichev.
29–30 September	Massacre at Babi Yar.
2 October	'Operation Typhoon' begins; 7000 Jews murdered in Mogilev.
7 October	Germans capture 650 000 Red Army soldiers at Vyazma.
16 October	Soviet government offices begin partial evacuation of Moscow.
20 October	7000 Jews murdered in Borisov.
24 October	Germans capture Kharkov.
13 November	German conference at Orsha where attack upon Moscow is decided.
30 November	26 000 Jews murdered in Riga by 8 December.
5 December	Red Army begins counterattacks at Moscow; these will coalesce into a major offensive within a few days.
8 December	Hitler orders the suspension of 'Typhoon' and defensive positions for the rest of the winter.
19 December	Brauchitsch relieved of command; Hitler assumes command of the Army.

1942

5 April	Directive for 'Operation Blue' is issued.
8 May	'Operation Blue' launched with attack on the Crimea.
30 May	Soviets create the Central Staff of the Partisan Movement.
28 June	Germans launch attack into the Caucasus region.
3 July	Germans capture Sevastopol.
26 August	Zhukov is made Stalin's chief deputy of the armed forces.
10 September	German forces enter Stalingrad.
19 November	Red Army launches counter-attack against flanks of German positions at Stalingrad ('Operation Uranus').
23 November	German forces in Stalingrad are surrounded.
12 December	Attempted relief of German forces in Stalingrad.

1943

3 January	Germans retreat from the Caucasus.
2 February	German forces at Stalingrad surrender.

16 February	Soviets recapture Kharkov.
15 March	Germans recapture Kharkov.
5 July	'Operation Citadel' begins.
12 July	Soviets launch numerous offensives in the Ukraine.
13 July	Hitler orders end of 'Operation Citadel'.
23 August	Soviets recapture Kharkov for the last time.
25 September	Red Army recaptures Smolensk.
6 November	Red Army recaptures Kiev.
24 December	Beginning of Soviet offensives across the Ukraine.

1944

26 January	German siege of Leningrad ends.
8 March	Hitler issues 'fortified places' order.
8 April	Red Army launches offensive into the Crimea.
22 June	Red Army launches 'Operation Bagration'.
4 July	Red Army recaptures Minsk.
24 July	Red Army captures Maidanek, the first death camp to be liberated.
17 August	Red Army reaches Prussian border.
19 September	Armistice ends the war between Finland and the USSR.
24 December	Budapest surrounded by Red Army.

1945

12 January	Soviet winter offensive launched.
17 January	Red Army captures Warsaw.
26 January	Red Army captures Auschwitz-Birkenau.
13 February	Budapest captured by the Red Army.
30 March	Red Army captures Danzig.
13 April	Red Army captures Vienna.
16 April	Red Army launches assault on Berlin.
25 April	Soviet and American forces meet near Torgau.
30 April	Hitler commits suicide in Berlin.
2 May	Red Army captures Berlin.
7 May	German armed forces unconditionally surrender to the Allies.
13 May	Remnants of Army Group Center surrender near Prague.

Who's Who

Bach Zelewski, Eric von dem (1899–1972): SS General and Police Leader, he was the chief of the anti-partisan units on the eastern front after July, 1943. He was also in command of crushing the Warsaw rising in the summer of 1944.

Bagramyan, Ivan (1897–1982): Soviet general who was one of the planners of the failed offensive to recapture Kharkov in 1942, one of the primary generals at Kursk, and was instrumental in the offensives after 'Operation Bagration,' especially in pinning Army Group North into the Courland and effectively destroying it.

Bock, Fedor von (1880–1945): Commander of Army Group Center from June 1941 until December 1941. In January 1942 he was given command of Army Group South for 'Operation Blue' until disagreements with Hitler led to his retirement in July 1942. Died when his car was strafed in May, 1945.

Brauchitsch, Walther von (1881–1948): Commander in chief of the German army from 1938 until his retirement in December 1941, when Hitler took over his position.

Busch, Ernst von (1885–1945): Field Marshal who commanded an army in June, 1941 and rose to command Army Group Center from November, 1943 until June, 1944.

Chuikov, Vasily (1900–1982): Soviet army commander responsible for the defense of Stalingrad. His forces also participated in the capture of Berlin in 1945 and he negotiated its surrender with the Germans.

Churchill, Winston (1874–1965): British Prime Minister from June, 1940 through the end of the war. His determined anti-Nazi stance was a morale booster during the worst crises of the early period of the war.

Göring, Hermann (1893–1946): Commander of the *Luftwaffe*, economic czar of Germany, and the designated successor to Hitler until April 1945.

Guderian, Heinz (1888–1954): One of the foremost Panzer specialists, Guderian commanded Second Panzer group of Army Group Center during 1941. His disagreements with Hitler led to his retirement in December 1941, but after the debacle at Stalingrad he was recalled as inspector of Panzer Troops. In July 1944 he was made Chief of the General Staff, but was dismissed after arguments with Hitler in March 1945.

Halder, Franz (1884–1972): Chief of the General Staff from 1938 until his dismissal in September 1942 after disagreements with Hitler about the diversion of forces to Stalingrad during 'Operation Blue.'

Heydrich, Reinhard (1904–42): Chief of domestic security, responsible for creating the mechanisms of the Holocaust, including the *Einsatzgruppen*, which he created and which reported to him. Assassinated by Czech agents.

Himmler, Heinrich (1900–1945): Head of the *SS* and chief of all German police. He was responsible for operating the concentration and death camps as well as directing the *Einsatzgruppen*.

Hitler, Adolf (1889–1945): Leader of Germany from 1933–45.

Hoth, Hermann (1885–1971): Commander of a panzer group during the early part of 'Barbarossa,' by 1942 he was the army commander who lost the second battle for Kharkov. He participated in 'Operation Blue' as a panzer army commander and led the attempt to relieve Stalingrad after it was surrounded. During the late summer of 1943 he was blamed for the spectacular advance of the Red Army in the Ukraine and fired by Hitler. He remained sidelined until the last weeks of the war.

Jodl, Alfred (1890–1946): Chief of the OKW operations staff from 1939 through the end of the war. A principal military advisor to Hitler, he was hanged after the Nuremberg War Crimes Trials.

Kleist, Ewald von (1881–1954): Commander of the First Panzer Group of Army Group South in June 1941. Participated in some of the largest operations on the Eastern Front, including leading the forces in the Caucasus during 'Operation Blue.' Relieved of command after his perceived failure to hold the Crimea in 1944.

Kluge, Günther von (1882–1944): As Field Marshal, he participated in the invasion of France in 1940 and spent the rest of his career on the Eastern Front. He was in command of Army Group Center from 1943–43. In 1944, Kluge replaced Rundstedt as commander of the Western Front. He committed suicide in August 1944.

Konev, Ivan (1897–1971): Soviet army commander who fought from the first days of June, 1941 in the area of Army Group Center. His armies launched the counterattack at Moscow in 1941 which stopped the Germans. He also took part in the battles of Kursk, Korsun, Kanev, Kharkov, and Berlin, which he is credited with capturing (also spelled Koniev).

Kuznetsov, Nikolai (1904–74): Commander of the Red Navy during the war, he was part of the highest leadership circles during the war.

Leeb, Wilhelm von (1876–1956): Commander of Army Group North from June 1941–January 1942, when he was retired.

List, Wilhelm (1880–1971): Commander of Army Group North during the initial invasion of the Soviet Union in 1941–42. He was dismissed from his post in 1942 and served in no other position during the war.

Manstein, Erich von (1887–1973): Panzer leader in Army Group North during 1941, he was moved to Army Group South to capture the Crimea. In September 1942 he was transferred to capture Leningrad, and in the fall moved to Army Group South again to save Sixth Army at Stalingrad. Placed in command of Army Group South, he conducted the withdrawals to the Dnepr until relieved of command in April 1944.

Marcks, Erich (1891–1944): General who wrote and submitted the first plan for 'Operation Barbarossa.' This plan formed the basis for subsequent plans and the final plan.

Model, Walther (1891–1945): Panzer divisional commander in June 1941, subordinate to Guderian. Army commander in Army Group Center until January 1944 when he was given command of Army Group North, and then Army Group South when Manstein was relieved. In June 1944 he was given command of Army Group Center as it collapsed under the blows of 'Operation Bagration' (thus leading two Army Groups at the same time). In August 1944 he was transferred to France, and committed suicide rather than face capture.

Molotov, Vyacheslav (1890–1986): Soviet minister for foreign affairs, he and Ribbentrop negotiated the Nazi–Soviet Pact of 1939.

Paulus, Friedrich (1890–1957): Commander of Sixth Army from January 1942, his task in 'Operation Blue' was to seize Stalingrad. Before the war he helped plan 'Operation Barbarossa.'

Pavlov, Dmitry (1897–1941): Red Army general and commander of West Front during the invasion in June, 1941. He bore the blame for his front's collapse and was shot.

Reichenau, Walther von (1884–1942): German Field Marshal who was a devoted adherent to the ideals of Nazism, he commanded Sixth Army (Army Group South) until November, 1941 when he succeeded Rundstedt as commander of Army Group South. He issued notoriously anti-Semitic orders to the troops of his army which were sent by Hitler to the other army commanders. Died of a heart attack.

Rokossovsky, Konstantin (1896–1968): Soviet army commander who participated in the defense of Moscow, the encirclement at Stalingrad, Kursk, 'Operation Bagration,' and the capture of Berlin.

Rundstedt, Gerd von (1875–1953): Commander of Army Group South from June 1941 until November, when he was relieved after the debacle at Rostov.

Stalin, Josef (1879–1953): The leader of the USSR. Born Iosif Vissarionovich Dzhugashvili, Stalin adopted this name during his days as communist revolutionary.

Timoshenko, Semyon (1895–1970): Held high ranking positions with the Red Army at various times, including *Front* commander during most of the major battles on the Eastern Front.

Vasilevsky, Alexander (1895–1977): Member of the Soviet general staff and army commander responsible for many of the largest operations during the war, including Stalingrad, Kursk, the liberation of the Crimea, and 'Operation Bagration.'

Vatutin, Nikolai (1901–44): One of the most capable of Soviet generals, during the early days of the war he fought against Army Group North and helped blunt its advance towards Leningrad. He served alternately as front commander and representative of *Stavka* to the various fronts. He participated in the battles of Kursk, Kharkov, and the recapture of Kiev. He was killed by Ukrainian partisans in the spring of 1944.

Voroshilov, Kliment (1881–1969): Red Army general, minister of defense before the war, and a member of the GKO.

Yeremenko, Andrei (1892–1970): *Front* commander who participated in most of the major operations of the Eastern Front.

Zhukov, Georgii (1896–1974): Deputy Supreme Commander of the Red Army, Zhukov was instrumental in most of the major Soviet operations during the war, including the defense of Moscow, Stalingrad, Leningrad, Kursk, the operations in 1944, and the assault on Berlin.

Glossary

Army: A military unit made up of several corps (often three), which consist of several divisions (often also three). An army could theoretically consist of nine divisions, although as the war progressed German armies usually had no more than around six. There were dozens of armies in both the German and Soviet armed forces. In German practice armies were combined into Army Groups, of which there were usually three in the east. The Soviets combined their armies into *fronts*.

Army Group: An armed force composed of several armies, which were in turn formed from corps, which in turn were formed of several divisions. In German usage an army group usually comprised 3–4 armies. During the fighting on the Eastern Front the Germans divided their forces into three army groups: North, Center, and South (South was split and given other names at various times).

Cauldron: When a military unit is surrounded and behind enemy lines it is said to be captured in a 'cauldron.' Many of the battles of the Eastern Front were cauldron battles.

Division: A military unit consisting of a few regiments made up of several battalions, and consisting of around, for the Germans, 12 000 men, and for the Soviets around 10 000 men. This was the smallest basic fighting unit on the eastern front, although as the war progressed the Germans often broke divisions up and used regiments for specific purposes.

Donbas: The Don and Donets river basin in the Ukraine. A rich industrial and agricultural area highly desired by both sides during the war.

Einsatzgruppen: Four mobile murder squads of approximately 500–1000 men each organized by Reinhard Heydrich. Their task was to round up and shoot communists, Jews, and anyone politically suspect behind the front lines. They were responsible for up to 1.5 million deaths on the eastern front.

Envelop: In military usage, a maneuver which encircles an enemy formation. A single envelopment occurs when an enemy flank is penetrated to encircle the entire unit from one side; a double envelopment is when both flanks are penetrated and the unit is surrounded from both sides.

Flank: In military usage this is the furthest area of a unit's zone of control on either side. Facing the enemy, there are two flanks: the left and right, and beyond these flanks there are no units controlled by the unit commander. This makes flanks vulnerable because the commanders on the spot do not have control over neighboring units which occupy the zones beyond their flanks and cannot as effectively protect their own men if an attack occurs there.

Front: In Soviet usage, a front was a group of armies (of various sizes) led and directed by a common headquarters and was roughly analogous to a German army group but much smaller. These were continually renamed and were called, for example, West Front, Stalingrad Front, etc. After the Red Army began liberating Soviet territory from the Germans they were numbered and given regional names, for example, First Belorussian Front. In general terms a front is the area at which fighting occurs between enemies.

GKO: Soviet State Committee of Defense, organized on 30 June and given broad nearly dictatorial powers over the USSR. It ran the war and country until 4 September 1945, two days after Japan surrendered.

Landsers: The German nickname for its infantry.

Lebensraum: The German idea that they needed 'living space' in eastern Europe. The common idea was that this space would be taken from the USSR.

Luftwaffe: The German air force, headed by Hermann Göring. It played a large role during the early days of the war but was gradually pushed from the skies.

OKH (*Oberkommando des Heeres*), Supreme Command of the Army: Its chief was Walther von Brauchitsch until December 1941, when Hitler took his place. It was responsible for operations on the Eastern Front.

OKW (*Oberkommando der Wehrmacht*), Supreme Command of the German Armed Forces: Its chief was Wilhelm Keitel. Responsible for all fronts except the Eastern Front, which was the responsibility of the OKH.

'*Operation Bagration:*' The Soviet codeword for the massive and overwhelmingly successful offensive against Army Group Center during the summer of 1944.

'*Operation Barbarossa:*' The German codeword for the invasion of the USSR in June, 1941.

'*Operation Blue:*' The German codeword for the offensive into the Caucasus and Stalingrad during the summer of 1942.

'*Operation Citadel:*' The German codeword for the offensive against the bulge at Kursk during the summer of 1943.

'*Operation Edelweiss:*' The German codeword for the invasion of the Caucasus region during 1942.

'*Operation Kutuzov:*' The Soviet operation against the northern neck of the Kursk bulge during the summer of 1943.

'*Operation Mars:*' The Soviet offensive against Army Group Center, November, 1942.

'*Operation Rumiantsev:*' The Soviet offensive against the southern neck of the Kursk bulge during the summer of 1943.

'*Operation Saturn:*' The Soviet operation against Rostov to eliminate Army Group A in the Caucasus during the early winter of 1942. It was modified into 'Little Saturn' after the Germans launched a relief effort to save the Sixth Army in Stalingrad.

'*Operation Typhoon:*' The German codeword for the assault against Moscow in the late fall of 1941.

'*Operation Uranus:*' The Soviet codeword for the offensive against Army Group B which resulted in the encirclement at Stalingrad.

Rasputitsa: Literally, the 'time without roads.' A Russian term to describe the rainy periods during the fall and spring when the roads became merely mud.

SS (Schutzstaffel): Literally, 'protective squad.' Led by Heinrich Himmler, the SS was responsible for administering and carrying out the Holocaust. A branch of the SS, the *Waffen SS*, served as combat units.

Stavka: The overall command of the Red Army. Its head was Stalin, and it consisted of various men over time, all top-ranking generals. Its members were often sent on missions to various fronts facing crises. Zhukov and Vasilevsky were Stavka representatives at various points of the war.

Wehrmacht: The German armed forces, including the army, navy, and air force.

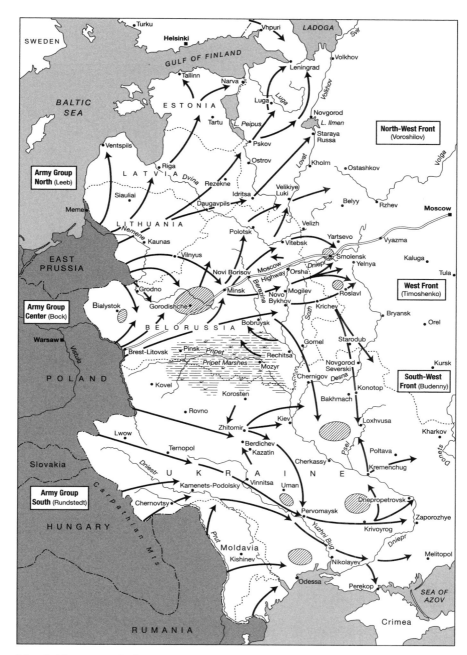

Map 1 'Operation Barbarossa,' June 1941

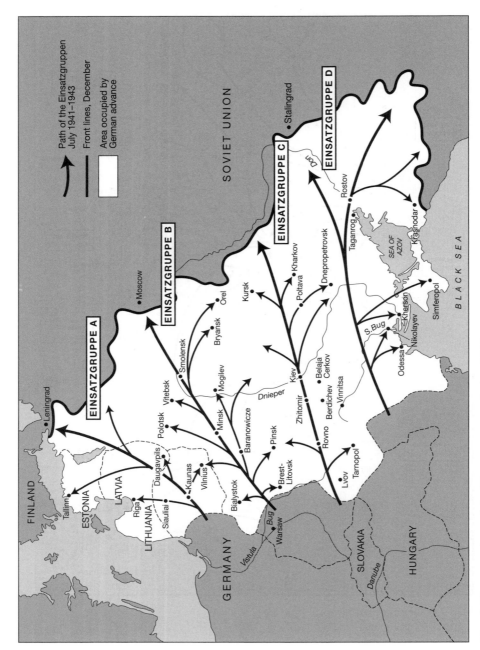

Map 2 The operations of the Einsatzgruppen during 1941

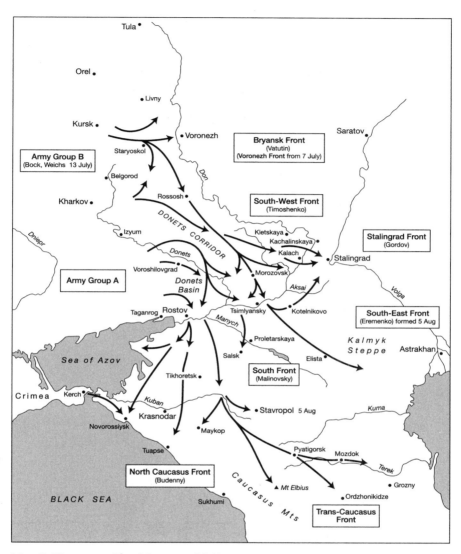

Map 3 'Operation Blue,' Summer 1942

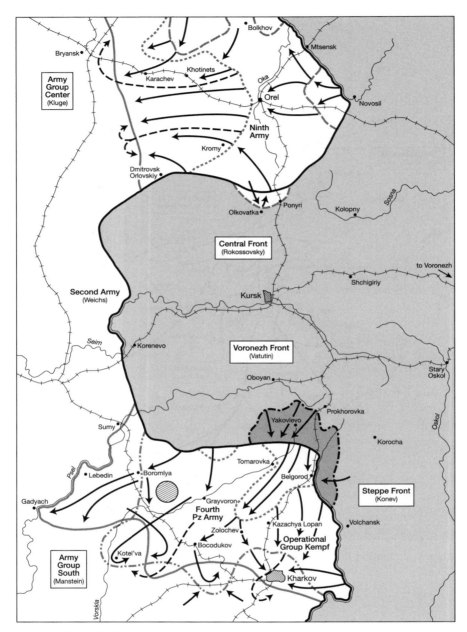

Map 4 The Battle for Kursk, July 1943

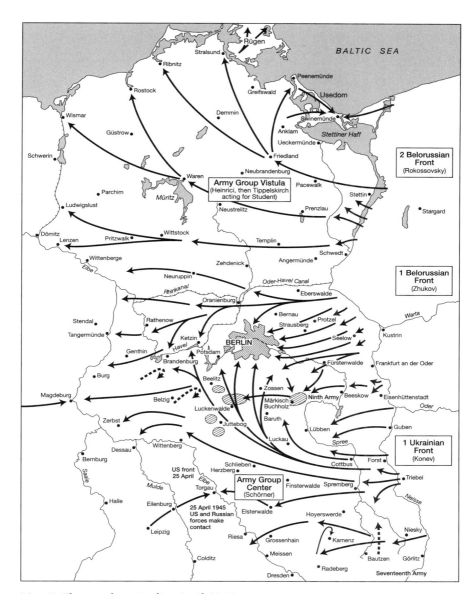

Map 5 The attack on Berlin, April 1945

Part 1

ANALYSIS

Introduction

On 22 June, 1941, barely a year after defeating the French army in a spectacular and astonishing demonstration of martial skills, the armed forces of Germany launched another massive invasion, this time against the Soviet Union. Code-named 'Operation Barbarossa', for many weeks it looked as if the easy victory over France would be repeated as millions of hapless Red Army soldiers were either taken prisoner or killed in one of the largest encirclement battles in history. German armored pincers rapidly encircled several of the Soviet Union's major western cities, including Brest-Litovsk, Minsk, and Smolensk, and within a month threatened Leningrad, Kiev, and even Moscow itself. Total Soviet collapse and German victory seemed certain within just a few weeks of the invasion. And yet the seemingly inevitable did not happen, and the front lines not only stabilized during the early fall but became relatively quiet, much to the relief of the Soviet leadership and its badly bludgeoned army. The short break proved, however, to be merely a brief pause so that the Germans could prepare fresh disasters for the Red Army. Early that fall the Germans launched a major offensive which swept virtually unopposed into the Ukraine, encircling Kiev and capturing over 600 000 prisoners. The carefully laid and massive trap consisted of an enormous pincer movement – the significance of which the Soviets completely failed to grasp. By the time autumn arrived the war was proving to be far more disastrous and dangerous for the Soviet state than even the most pessimistic assessments had predicted.

Before the invasion Germany was at war only with England, which had (along with France) declared war after the German invasion of Poland in September, 1939. With 'Operation Barbarossa' Germany faced, for the second time in a generation, a major war on two fronts, a prospect which had proven beyond German capabilities during the First World War when, despite defeating Tsarist Russia in the field, Germany's economic exhaustion prevented it from achieving victory on the Western Front. No one, least of all the Germans, believed the country could emerge victorious from another two-front war, and the German decision to attack the USSR in 1941 thus came as a surprise to most of the world, especially the Soviet leadership. Despite the serious risks associated with a two-front war, few international observers doubted a rather rapid collapse of the Red Army (American intelligence services foresaw a Soviet collapse within two months), while German operational planning anticipated it within a matter of weeks.

That total Soviet collapse did not occur, and that the Germans ultimately suffered catastrophic defeat has been the pivot around which studies of the war have revolved ever since the fighting began. Over the years scholars have put forward, with various degrees of success, just about every imaginable thesis for the war's genesis and course. There has never been a central or dominant viewpoint, and the foci of research have thus varied from the personalities involved – especially Adolf Hitler's reckless megalomania and Stalin's equally ruthless paranoia – to German and Soviet preparations for war, including flawed strategic and economic planning on both sides, and an insufficient German material buildup for the invasion. Even such seemingly mundane factors as the weather have been enrolled as explanatory causes for German defeat, especially at certain 'key' battles.

But an interpretation of the war which adequately includes the incredible variety of factors at play in the east has proven to be elusive. Attempts to make sense of the war have emphasized the systemic flaws within the German strategic command structures, especially the ways in which the German command appears to have ossified and hindered rather than encouraged a successful approach to the war. Other scholars have focused on the philosophical and political issues associated with conquering the vast lands of the Soviet Union and integrating them into the resources of the Reich. Thus the natural friction which accompanies military conquest was made worse by the divergent economic, political, and racial goals of competing German agencies such as the SS, the army, and the various economic ministries charged with exploiting the conquered resources and peoples in the east. There was never, for example, a single German ministry with the overall authority to extract the precious resources, but rather a multiplicity of competing agencies interested primarily in acquiring materials for themselves.

Previous approaches to the war thus looked at particular pieces of the puzzle rather than taking a holistic approach, which meant that individual features came into focus but that an overall perspective which addressed the salient issues was difficult to assemble. For example, none of the early analyses provided answers to important questions about the role of Hitler's peculiar social-Darwinist racist ideology in the formulation of German operational plans. There has not even been, until recently, a remotely adequate explanation as to why Stalin and Hitler agreed upon a mutual non-aggression treaty just days prior to the German invasion of Poland and its relationship to Hitler's decision to attack his putative ally. Previous explanations which viewed it as simple opportunism on the part of both men now seem too simplistic and leave too many questions unanswered.

Recent scholarship tries to address the various problems and omissions associated with earlier views by broadening the scope of the analysis of the war to include not just military history, which naturally has its limitations, but also the social, political, and economic factors which played important roles for both the German invaders and Soviet defenders. These works have examined so many disparate aspects of the war which had hitherto been ignored that our understanding has broadened to the point where a comprehensive perspective which takes into account the intentions and actions of both the German and Soviet participants, including civilians and the home front is becoming feasible. It is no longer sufficient to see the war as simply an attempt by the Germans to dominate Europe; German intentions actually went much further than traditional great power politics. It is now becoming clear that German goals in the east included not merely conquest of the vast and fertile lands of the western Soviet Union, but the erection of an eastern European racial empire based upon Hitler's ideas about racial struggle as the keystone of human development. The core of his conception was the conquest of living space in the east for resettlement by German colonists. Hitler was not simply trying to reestablish Germany's position in Europe as one of its great powers, but instead attempting to forge something which had never existed before: a racial state intent upon acquiring for itself the living space which it felt it required for its continued existence. These goals were to be accomplished at the expense, labor, and lives of the various ethnic peoples of the USSR, especially its Jews, Poles, and Ukrainians. This focus on the racial aspect of the war has now assumed center stage and is a crucial key in understanding both the genesis and the incredible violence of the war.

The eventual catastrophic German defeat after so many early and relatively easy victories has also caused its share of controversy: how and why did the Germans lose the war? Did the vaunted German army take the task seriously? Did racial bias and prejudice against Slavs prevent an honest assessment of Soviet capabilities and blind German planners to the very real dangers of an invasion? Were the seeds of defeat therefore planted long before the first shots had even been fired? Or was planning sufficient but, after losing several 'turning point' battles, such as those at Stalingrad or Kursk, was the German war machine so physically battered that it could neither replenish itself materially nor re-conceptualize a new approach to the war? How early in the war can signs of German collapse be seen and, conversely, how late in the war could the Germans have snatched victory from defeat? At what point can we see that the Soviets would most likely win the war? These questions go to the crux of the significance of the Eastern Front: at what point did the

USSR become a world super-power? What role did the war play in the rise of the USSR to the status of major world power and the dominant power in eastern Europe for decades after 1945? When, in other words, did the Red Army cease being a 'stumbling colossus' and become a force to be reckoned with?

Compounding these questions is the degree to which the Red Army was ready for war in 1941 or whether its performance had been compromised due to the purges of the 1930s. There can be little doubt that the Red Army performed very poorly during the opening phases of the invasion as many of its disastrous early defeats were more often the result of its own incompetence rather than German superiority. The inability to fight effectively permeated the command structures and there was an apparent inability to coordinate, at all levels, even the simplest unit movements and the most elementary offensive and defensive maneuvers. Many units could not even construct adequate trench systems, erect effective fire zones, or lay minefields. This failure to create an effective defensive posture at even the most elementary level looms large in the histories of the early phases of the war and must be explained if we are to understand the evolution of the Red Army from master bungler to master of much of Europe within just a few years.

Some of the early Soviet failures have been blamed upon Stalin's attitude concerning a possible German attack. Before the war began various foreign leaders, including Franklin Roosevelt and Winston Churchill, forwarded intelligence which revealed German troop movements to the east and a massive buildup of war materiel close to Soviet borders. Stalin and the Soviet military leadership chose to ignore these legitimate and accurate warnings about the impending invasion primarily, it now seems, because Stalin simply refused to accept that Hitler would open a second front while still engaged in a war with England. He therefore regarded all reports about a possible invasion, regardless of the source, as provocations designed to lead the Soviet Union into joining the war on England's side and thus, as he put it, to pull England's chestnuts from the fire. He was convinced, even during the hours after the invasion began, that it was irrational for Hitler to attack in the east until the war with England was settled, and his policies from 1939–41 flowed from this deeply held belief. His convictions had the fateful consequence that, since Soviet military doctrine emphasized offensive rather than defensive operations, the Red Army was deployed in offensive echelons rather than defensive positions when the invasion began. Some have argued that this aggressive posture meant that Stalin intended, at some future date of his choosing (1942 or 1943), to launch an invasion of western Europe, but that the German onslaught preempted his plan for the conquest of western Europe. This theory, that Hitler launched a 'preventive war' designed to prevent an eventual Soviet attack on European civilization dovetails with

German propaganda after 1943, but seems most unlikely given recent research. The most likely explanation for the poor performance of the Red Army in 1941, as shocking as it may seem for a nation's defense forces, was that it was caught unprepared to fight defensive warfare; to put it simply, the Red Army was not prepared for an invasion.

As the German armed forces swept into the Soviet Union they were engaged not only in the traditional tasks associated with all invasion forces, such as seizing bridges, strong points, and destroying the enemy's ability to resist, but also with political goals which originated within the racist ideology of both Hitler and the head of the SS, Heinrich Himmler. In particular, the army was to assist special units under Himmler's control. These special forces, or *Einsatzgruppen*, were tasked by Himmler with locating and eliminating potential sources of trouble behind the front lines through mass shootings, especially of captured Communist party officials, but also male civilian Jews who had committed no offense, wore no uniform, and were not Communist party members. The army was responsible for ensuring that these units, which numbered a few thousand men in total, not only had access to the facilities and equipment necessary to carry out their assignments but ensuring that regular army units in no way interfered with the completion of their tasks. As the armored spearheads sliced through the Soviet countryside they were closely followed by these murder squads everywhere along the front (each army group had been assigned its own task force). Earlier in the year Hitler had explained to his top generals that this was to be a war of 'annihilation' and that the army was expected to carry out its part in the 'great tasks' which lay ahead. Thus the mass murders which took place during the summer and fall of 1941 did so in the presence and with the complicity of the German armed forces; the brutal massacre of over 30 000 Jews at Kiev in September, 1941, must therefore be seen within the context of the rapid and broad advance of the *Wehrmacht* into the Soviet Union; German military victories made such brutality possible. Until recently the link between military operations and the activities of the murder squads has been de-emphasized, but the two must be seen as two sides of the same coin: total racial and political war against the peoples of the USSR.

The battles fought to achieve this racial victory have given rise to controversies of their own. The idea that at certain stages of the war German victory was still possible has led to the conception of 'turning points' moments when German victory was snatched away by defeat, often through massive Soviet offensives. The battle for Stalingrad has played a central role in this concept largely because up to that point the Germans appeared to be winning the war. But therein lies the trouble with the idea of turning points: if Stalingrad really was the turning point of the war, then what is the significance of the grievous defeat before Moscow during 1941–42? Was that battle a turning point? What criteria should be used in determining whether a battle was a turning point, and could there have been multiple turning points? If so, does this not devalue the concept to the point of meaninglessness? The question over which battle was the precise moment when the war was lost for the Germans is unanswerable and can lead only to sterile debate about inconsequential issues. Recently a more balanced view has been adopted wherein there is the explicit recognition that a myriad of contingent historical forces were at play which no contemporary could sort through (and, indeed, which is proving difficult to analyze more than 60 years later). Perhaps there were no turning points because the Germans never really had a chance for a clear-cut victory. It could be that the best outcome for the Germans all along would have been some kind of partial strategic victory which might have given Hitler the political space he needed to negotiate a peace settlement (an extremely unlikely scenario given his opinions). The nature of a possible German victory, whether partial or total, has long dominated studies of the war. By 1944, however, most observers recognize that there was no longer any hope of German victory, even a negotiated one, as German forces simply began to disintegrate in the face of several major and concerted Soviet offensives all along the front.

One of the more active research topics has been the history of resistance movements in eastern Europe, in particular the role played by partisans in the final Soviet victory. The debate over whether or not they made significant contributions to the war effort, or in fact became merely an exercise in Soviet propaganda, is a debate which will never be resolved to anyone's satisfaction. Did the partisans contribute to final victory or cause additional casualties which might have been avoided had the Germans not feared for their lives and supply lines behind the front? The partisan war, which looms large in recent historiography, is an important element in explaining both the level of violence and the German failure to erect adequate security measures behind the front lines. This omission is thus indicative of larger German failures in the east, as it is a reflection of the overall German failure to prepare adequately for the type of total war they had both envisioned and planned from the very beginning.

In glaring contrast to the humiliating defeats inflicted upon the Red Army during the first two years of the war, the last two witnessed outstanding feats of Soviet arms. The contrast between the hapless Soviet armies crushed at Kiev in 1941 and the hapless German armies crushed in Minsk in June, 1944 can hardly be more dramatic; by the summer of 1944 the Soviets practiced an outstanding version of an operational art of warfare far beyond German capabilities to either emulate or counter. The development of this Soviet juggernaut, aimed right at the heart of Germany and determined to destroy the 'fascist beast,' had a profound impact upon the political development of post-war Europe and the world. No longer could the power of the Soviet Union be dismissed as of little value; one of the ironies of the war of the Eastern Front is that it made the Soviet Union one of the post-war arbiters of world affairs. The war, in other words, brought the USSR into play as an international actor for the first time in its history, and its results continue to reverberate throughout the world today.

The war on the Eastern Front was, and remains, without parallel in world history. It claimed the lives of tens of millions and left major Soviet cities in ruins. At once a racial war, a political war, and a war for European empire, it consumed more material resources than any before and left both physical and political scars which have still not fully healed. To the loss of lives must be added the destruction of property, economies, and political systems across eastern Europe. That such a world-shattering event occurred boggles the imagination, and the purpose of this volume is not only to explain how and why it happened, but to examine the historical circumstances surrounding it to determine its historical significance.

1

The Background

THE ORIGINS OF THE WAR ON THE EASTERN FRONT

At 03:00 on the morning of 22 June 1941, German aircraft began bombing Soviet airfields and communications sites all along their common border from the Baltic to the Black seas. The bombing, which was largely unopposed, destroyed a large portion of the Soviet air force on the ground as well as cutting critical communication networks. These strikes were designed to blind the Red Army so that it would be unable to respond effectively as events unfolded along the border. Fifteen minutes later German artillery opened fire upon Soviet army positions, and 15 minutes after the artillery fire began German tank and infantry units leaped across the Soviet border. An hour later the German ambassador to the Soviet Union informed the Soviet foreign minister that Germany had invaded the Soviet Union. The largest and most destructive war in the history of warfare had begun.

The war on the Eastern Front was unlike any other conflict in recorded history. In addition to the usual economic and political factors which contribute to the outbreak of war, the German invasion of the USSR was based upon ideological premises which set it apart from previous wars. Its enormous scale also marked it as a departure in warfare, as it dwarfed even the mass offensives of the First World War. The number of men and the amount of materiel devoted to its prosecution were unprecedented, as well as the distances covered by the combatants (which were far larger than those of the Western Front in either world war). The economic resources both sides devoted to the war were the most thoroughly mobilized of any belligerents up to that point in history. Millions of Soviet and German soldiers and civilians were killed, wounded, or captured during the course of the nearly four-year war, and many of the most populous and important Soviet and eastern German cities were either captured or threatened, including almost all of European Russia.

In pursuit of their agenda in the USSR, the Germans drew up economic and domestic policies which envisioned the total exploitation of both its natural resources and its people. But this war was not only about economic resources and who had the right to utilize them, it was also a racial war of the German 'Aryans' against the Slavic 'sub-humans,' as Nazi propaganda portrayed the citizens of the Soviet Union. In order to clear the way for the economic colonization of the USSR on a previously unknown scale, German units were assigned the task of not only conquering vast amounts of Soviet territory but mass murder; the war was to eradicate both the political and, in German eyes, racial enemies of the German people: communists, Slavs, and Jews. The war on the Eastern Front was a war of annihilation of one European people against other European peoples.

The origins of a war of such monumental proportions, code named '**Operation Barbarossa**,' are still a matter of considerable debate. Germany and the Soviet Union had enjoyed fairly cordial relations during the 1920s and had cooperated on military matters when both were pariahs within the western world. This friendship ended when **Adolf Hitler**, an outspoken anti-communist throughout his political career, became the chancellor of Germany in January 1933. For him communism was not merely an odious political ideology but a Jewish conspiracy whose goal was to conquer the world. He therefore could not permit continuing relations with a nation he considered a 'Judeo-Bolshevik' state and contacts and cooperation between the two nations dwindled rather rapidly to insignificant levels. During the remainder of the 1930s the two states had no relations of any substantive nature, neither friendly nor overtly hostile.

All of this changed on 23 August 1939 when the two nations surprised everyone by signing a non-aggression pact. Politics makes, as the saying goes, strange bedfellows and both **Josef Stalin** and Hitler had what they believed were sound political reasons for reaching an agreement. For the Soviets the pact represented security and stability in eastern Europe, something they had been trying to ensure throughout the 1930s (the USSR joined the League of Nations in 1934). The USSR had tried to contain aggressive German posturing during the 1930s through multilateral action in conjunction with France and Britain, but the West had proven to be unresponsive and Soviet efforts failed to have any result. By 1938 Stalin was convinced that the Western Allies were more interested in appeasing Hitler than stopping him, and his beliefs were reinforced during the crisis over Czechoslovakia in September 1939. The Soviet Union had promised to make troops available to the Czechs and partly mobilized the Red Army when the crisis erupted, but when France and Britain agreed to German demands that the country be dismembered at the Munich Conference (to which the USSR had not been invited), Stalin concluded that the West was more interested in anti-communism than

'Operation Barbarossa:' The German codeword for the invasion of the USSR in June, 1941.

Hitler, Adolf (1889–1945): Leader of Germany from 1933–45.

Stalin, Josef (1879–1953): The leader of the USSR. Born Iosif Vissarionovich Dzhugashvili, Stalin adopted this name during his days as communist revolutionary.

standing up to Hitler. The German betrayal of the Munich Pact in March 1939, however, finally made it clear to the French and British that assistance from the USSR was necessary if German expansionist policies were to be contained. The Soviets again offered an alliance to the West in April 1939, and early that August a military delegation from both nations was invited to Moscow for talks about the possibilities for an alliance. But the Western Allies made serious diplomatic errors, including sending the delegates by ship rather than flying; their lengthy ocean voyage gave the Soviets the impression that the West was in no hurry to reach an agreement. Once the delegates had finally arrived the Soviets were shocked to discover that they were relatively low ranking officers who were not empowered to sign binding documents. During the ensuing talks the British and French delegates claimed not to know their governments' positions on so many vital aspects of the negotiations and had such little authority that the Soviets immediately concluded that the West was not truly interested in forming an alliance. The final blow to these negotiations came when the British offered only 16 divisions as their part of the coalition, a figure the Soviets considered so ridiculously low (but in reality a stretch for the British) that they concluded the alliance was pointless and sent the delegation home. Collective security with the West, from the viewpoint of the Soviets, was a dead issue (Carley, 1999).

Within a few days of this diplomatic fiasco the Germans were in Moscow ironing out the details of a joint non-aggression pact. Hitler sent Stalin a personal letter on 20 August asking him to receive the German foreign minister, Joachim von Ribbentrop, no later than 23 August, in order to work out the details of a Soviet–German agreement. It is now generally agreed that Hitler concluded the pact with his long-time ideological enemy because he wanted to ensure there would not be a two-front war while he pursued a military solution against Poland. He hoped that the pact with the USSR would separate it from the West diplomatically and force the Western powers to rethink declaring war on Germany in support of Poland. It was a political calculation designed to limit the extent of the war, as Hitler wished to prevent France and Britain from seeking an alliance with the Soviet Union and creating a two-front war (Fleischhauer, 1997). His ideas about the USSR had not changed or mellowed; the pact was a temporary expedient given the political and diplomatic circumstances.

Stalin apparently hoped that by coming to terms with Hitler he could achieve peace for the USSR. Germany, he hoped, would never turn against the east if it became bogged down in a war against France and Britain; such a war would, most likely, be a replay of the stalemate of the First World War and either permanently preoccupy Germany in the west or weaken it to the point where it could do nothing militarily in the east. Either way, the USSR would be free to pursue an aggressive agenda in the Balkans and the straits leading to the Mediterranean Sea without German interference (Murphy, 2005). Some scholars have concluded that Stalin hoped the war would be another long and exhausting one which would lead to a peace conference at which the USSR, since it would be the only European power not exhausted by war, could extract substantial concessions (Gorodetsky, 1999). Whether this is true or not, it is nonetheless clear that both men made the pact while pursuing their own interests. The Soviets made the pact in order to buy time; the pact was, after the collapse of efforts to reach an Anglo-French agreement, the only viable diplomatic option available to the USSR (Fleischhauer, 1997). The Germans made the pact in order to prevent the impending invasion of Poland from turning into a war between them and France and Britain. The motivating factors which brought Hitler and Stalin together in a pact was not ideology but rather a sense of *realpolitik* which both thought best served their nations' interests.

The agreement [**Doc. 1, p. 110**] not only bound the two countries to a non-aggression pact but created mechanisms for peaceful economic relations. It made possible at least a partial resumption of the friendly relations the two nations had enjoyed during the 1920s, and the Soviet Union began almost immediately to provide raw materials, including grain, coal, and zinc, in exchange for sophisticated technological products from Germany. These economic agreements, such as the treaty of 10 January 1941 by which the USSR agreed to provide oil, fabrics, various metals, as well as agricultural goods such as grain and lumber, were very valuable to the German economy. By June 1941 the Soviets had delivered over 630 000 tons of grain, almost 250 000 tons of crude oil, 50 000 tons of manganese ore, nearly a ton of platinum, and about 25 000 tons of cotton, among other goods. In return the industrial goods the Germans provided to the USSR included a cruiser for the Soviet navy, the *Lutzov* (which was never delivered) (Bellamy, 2007: 95–7).

The pact thus made it possible for Germany to obtain vital raw materials and for the Soviets to obtain modern industrial technology neither could obtain elsewhere. But perhaps the most important aspect of the pact was the secret provisions which divided Poland into spheres of German and Soviet influence; everything east of the Narev, Vistula, and San rivers was in the Soviet sphere. A week after the pact was signed and made public the Germans invaded Poland, and on 3 September the Second World War began when both France and Britain declared war on Germany after it refused to withdraw its forces from Poland. On 17 September the USSR, observing the terms of the secret provisions of the pact, invaded its sphere in eastern Poland. The independent nation of Poland, which had been created in the aftermath of the First World War from parts of the Russian, German, and Austro-Hungarian empires, completely disappeared.

The pact, made by ideological enemies for specific diplomatic purposes, has been called a 'double deception' because Stalin was deceived twice: once by Hitler into thinking the pact ensured a lengthy period of peace for the USSR, and once by himself, as he was convinced that Hitler would never create a two-front war by invading the Soviet Union as long as the war in the west continued (Barros and Gregor, 1995). As long as Germany remained at war with Britain, Stalin felt safe. But this was self-delusional, as Hitler never intended to honor the pact (or any other written agreement) when it no longer served his purposes, even if Britain had not yet been defeated. The opportunity to discard the pact, which Hitler later said had been 'very irksome' to him, came with the defeat of France in 1940.

On 22 June 1940, the French government signed an armistice with Germany and ended one of the most outstanding feats of German military art. Once the French had been defeated and the British army had been evacuated at Dunkirk, the Germans controlled Europe from the Atlantic to the borders of the Soviet Union and from Norway to the shores of the Mediterranean Sea. Yet this victory, paradoxically, presented the Germans with a dilemma: how could they bring the war to a successful conclusion? The defeat of France reduced the combatants to Germany and Britain, but during the summer of 1940 the British (especially **Winston Churchill**) stubbornly refused to consider terms with the Germans. The only way they could force the British out of the war would have been to invade the island nation, but this was a hazardous undertaking which no one, not even Hitler, fully supported. At a meeting on 30 June 1940, **Alfred Jodl**, chief of the command staff of the Supreme Command of the Armed Forces (**OKW**) and one of Hitler's principal military advisors, presented three options for forcing Britain out of the war: initiate an air war against Britain in order to destroy British morale and persuade the British government to agree to a negotiated peace; prepare for an invasion if the bombing failed to achieve the desired goal; or attack Britain's overseas colonies to either lose them or agree to a negotiated peace. Hitler, characteristically, chose all three options. Throughout the summer of 1940 the 'Battle of Britain' was waged to force Britain either to capitulate or prepare the ground for a successful invasion. At the same time elaborate plans were worked out by the army staffs in preparation for the invasion of Britain, which had been given the code name 'Operation Sea Lion.' Hitler ultimately decided for a limited adoption of the third option by agreeing to plans for the seizure of Gibraltar and other key British Mediterranean bases such as Crete. The Germans therefore took a multi-faceted approach to ending the war with Britain after the defeat of France during the summer of 1940.

Hitler, however, had his own ideas about how to force Britain to end the war. **Franz Halder**, the chief of the Army general staff (**OKH**), recorded a

Churchill, Winston (1874–1965): British Prime Minister from June, 1940 through the end of the war. His determined anti-Nazi stance was a morale booster during the worst crises of the early period of the war.

Jodl, Alfred (1890–1946): Chief of the OKW operations staff from 1939 through the end of the war. A principal military advisor to Hitler, he was hanged after the Nuremberg War Crimes Trials.

OKW (*Oberkommando der Wehrmacht*), Supreme Command of the German Armed Forces: Its chief was Wilhelm Keitel. Responsible for all fronts except the Eastern Front, which was the responsibility of the OKH.

Halder, Franz (1884–1972): Chief of the General Staff from 1938 until his dismissal in September 1942 after disagreements with Hitler about the diversion of forces to Stalingrad during 'Operation Blue.'

OKH (*Oberkommando des Heeres*), Supreme Command of the Army: Its chief was Walther von Brauchitsch until December 1941, when Hitler took his place. It was responsible for operations on the Eastern Front.

meeting on 21 July 1940 at which Hitler claimed that the British 'puts hope in Russia' and that Germany must therefore 'tackle' the Russian problem and 'crush the Russian army' in order to deprive Britain of its last possible ally on the continent. On 31 July Halder recorded another meeting at which Hitler said that 'Russia is the factor on which Britain is relying the most,' and that 'with Russia smashed, Britain's last hope would be shattered.' Hitler announced that 'Russia's destruction must therefore be made a part of this struggle. Spring 1941' (Halder, 1988: 244). No one at this meeting disagreed with Hitler's estimation of British hopes or of the necessity of destroying the USSR. The views of Hitler and the top military leaders of Germany overlapped as far as a desire to move eastward. At least some of Germany's military elite had long looked towards the east for German expansion; during the First World War Field Marshal Paul von Hindenburg and General Erich Ludendorff created ambitious plans for the annexation of vast areas of western Russia after the collapse of the tsarist armies. Hitler had long held views that envisioned expansion towards the east, and war with the USSR provided a way to combine diplomatic and ideological considerations into a victorious strategy.

It is paradoxical that none of the military services, including those in Germany, Britain and the United States, felt the USSR possessed a viable or effective army in 1940, yet Hitler felt Britain hoped to survive the war because of Soviet arms. He believed that it was easier to drive Britain out of the war not by directly attacking its homeland, which he believed was extremely risky militarily and politically, but indirectly by invading the USSR, defeating it and making clear to the British that Europe offered no possibility of assistance. With all possible European allies thus either conquered or allied with Germany, Britain would have no choice but to end the war. In the balance of world powers the USSR was given, by Hitler, little value except as a crutch upon which the British could lean in these desperate times. Hitler therefore hoped to end the war with Britain by depriving it of its last possible ally in Europe and at the same time accomplishing several economic, political, and ideological goals at once. This decision has been called the 'turn to the east.'

Hitler believed he could end the war which had begun in September 1939 not by directly attacking the only other belligerent but by expanding the war and attacking a neutral third party which up to that point had continued to provide important raw materials under the terms of the economic agreements made after the Nazi–Soviet Pact. Compounding this tortuous logic is the plain fact that the USSR was not at war with Germany in 1940, had in fact made an alliance with it in August 1939, and it was unclear exactly how Britain could persuade the USSR to go to war with Germany as an British ally. After the disastrous Anglo-French mission to Moscow in August 1939 there had been no discussions between the British and the Soviets at any level about the possibility of the USSR entering the war against Germany. In fact, Churchill (who had been appointed Prime Minister during the final German assault upon France) actively pinned his hopes not on the USSR, which would have been abhorrent to this life-long anti-communist, but on the United States. But Hitler time and again clung to this belief, and in a letter on 21 June 1941 to Benito Mussolini [**Doc. 2, p. 110**], Hitler reiterated his contention that the Soviet Union was a prop by which Britain remained in the war and the invasion was thus a preemptive strike designed to prevent Britain from bringing the USSR into the war.

Few historians give any credence to Hitler's interpretation of the turn to the east. There is simply too much evidence that the Germans did not expect or fear an attack by the Soviet Union. The explanation of why the Germans invaded the USSR now centers on the racial expansionist policy inherent in Hitler's world-view. The core of Hitler's foreign policy was expansion to the east and it was his intention from the very beginning of his political career to invade the Soviet Union. The apparent continuity from *Mein Kampf*, Hitler's quasi-autobiography written during the mid-1920s, through a speech in 1937 during which Hitler announced to his generals the plan to find 'living space' (**lebensraum**) in the east, reinforces the idea that expansion eastward was a central tenet of his political ideology. In *Mein Kampf* and what is known as his *Second Book*, Hitler laid out a plan by which he believed Germany could achieve its proper place among the European super-powers (Hitler, 1943 and 2003). Foremost among his ideas was that German foreign policy had erred in forming an alliance with Austria-Hungary and Italy before the First World War. He believed the only viable foreign policy was for Germany to seek colonies not abroad but in the European east. He wrote that 'if we speak of new land in Europe today, we can primarily have in mind only Russia and her vassal border states,' and the only way to gain this 'new' living space was to destroy the Soviet Union which, to make matters worse from Hitler's viewpoint, was also communist. By invading the USSR Germany could crush an ideological and racial enemy (Hitler equated communism with Jews) and acquire fertile territory for Germanic settlement. Hitler thus desired a war against the USSR from the very beginning of his political career and in fact war in the east was the linchpin around which the rest of his domestic and foreign policies flowed (Jäckel, 1981).

The theme of a preemptive strike, raised in the letter to Mussolini and in a radio speech shortly after the war began, nonetheless remained a dominant German propaganda theme throughout the war. During the 1980s this thesis was again raised by a defector from the Soviet Union who published under the pseudonym of Victor Suvorov. According to his thesis, the Soviet Union planned a war against a western Europe dominated by Nazi Germany.

Lebensraum: The German idea that they needed 'living space' in eastern Europe. The common idea was that this space would be taken from the USSR.

Stalin hoped that Germany would serve as an 'ice breaker' by attacking the western democracies and would become bogged down in a grueling war reminiscent of the First World War. The Red Army would then, after adequate preparation, swoop down on the exhausted capitalist nations and defeat them in a rapid war. Suvorov, who claimed he had access to certain secret documents from the archives of the Red Army (which have never been found by subsequent researchers), claimed that the Soviets intended to attack Germany in 1941 or 1942 but had been forestalled by the German attack (Suvorov, 1990). His thesis, which echoes Hitler's view of an aggressive Soviet Union, has been rejected by most historians. Recently, another Russian historian has argued that the Red Army did indeed have a preemptive war in mind during 1941, but that it was theoretical and its planning and implementation were never completed and therefore that the USSR had no plans to invade Germany (Pleshakov, 2005). David Glantz, who has provided one of the more convincing criticisms of the 'ice breaker' thesis, explicitly demonstrated that the Soviets had no such plans and would in any event have been incapable of carrying them out for a long time (Glantz and House, 1995). No one now believes that the Soviets intended or possessed a plan to invade Germany in 1941 or 1942, but, as we shall see, the Red Army did possess an offensive military doctrine which believed that any war should be fought on enemy territory.

The 'turn to the east' therefore had little to do with Britain seeking an ally in the USSR, nor was it a preventive war; it was instead Hitler's intention all along. The declaration of war by France and Britain in September 1939 complicated his foreign policy plans as he did not want a war against them, and he spent the summer of 1940 trying to find a way out of this dilemma. The defeat of France during June 1940 made the possibility of peace with Britain more likely and therefore would permit the turn to the east, but Hitler needed to demonstrate that Britain could no longer rely upon or find allies on the continent. An invasion of the USSR before the conclusion of the war with Britain would enable Hitler to use the unique political and diplomatic situation after the defeat of France to link his ideological goals with the strategic necessity of defeating Britain. 'Operation Barbarossa' thus solved strategic problems which arose in the wake of the invasion of Poland and at the same time created the possibility of achieving Hitler's goals for *lebensraum* in the east (Förster, 1997). The invasion was thus politically expedient in that it created the conditions for achieving multiple German strategic goals (Robertson, 1989).

The timeless conflict between Germany and Russia over access to the Balkans also played an important role in leading to war; as Soviet pressure in the Balkans and the Baltic states alarmed the German military leadership their ideas merged with those of Hitler to create a symbiosis which favored war in the east. This synthesis meant that both Hitler and his generals could agree that 'Operation Barbarossa' was not only feasible but desirable. The German generals were thus as deeply involved in promoting the invasion of the USSR as Hitler, although they proceeded from different bases. The combination of a desire to resist Soviet encroachments in eastern Europe, a desire to defeat Britain, and Hitler's ultimate desire to turn east for ideological purposes laid the foundations which made 'Operation Barbarossa' possible. Thus an otherwise intelligent man such as the German Field Marshal **Gerd von Rundstedt** could claim after the war that the Soviets intended to attack Germany when it became bogged down in a war against the western powers and that 'Operation Barbarossa' was therefore an absolute military necessity.

Rundstedt, Gerd von (1875–1953): Commander of Army Group South from June 1941 until November, when he was relieved after the debacle at Rostov.

PLANNING 'OPERATION BARBAROSSA'

Until recently views of the war on the Eastern Front were dominated by the German interpretation. The Cold War between the West and the USSR meant that western historians did not have access to the mass of German documentation captured by the Red Army, or to Soviet documents and eyewitness accounts. In addition, the mountain of documentation captured from the Germans by the Western Allies at the end of the war provided a great deal of information about the Eastern Front, but from the German viewpoint. These documents, as well as the views expressed by the German officers and soldiers who published their memoirs after the war, played a major role in the way historians interpreted the war in the east during the years before the collapse of the USSR. Generally, these documents and memoirs spawned the view that the **Wehrmacht** had conducted a 'clean' war on the Eastern Front, that it fought the war just like any other army would have, and that any crimes that may have been committed had been carried out by the **SS**. In this view the army simply followed orders, just as military doctrine and discipline required. The lack of documentation on operations by both German and Soviet units on the Eastern Front meant that the initial histories of the war focused on military planning and operations but neglected to integrate racial goals and policies into their narratives. This arbitrary and unconscious division between military operations and serial murder has echoed throughout the years in numerous military histories which offer exceptionally detailed discussions of military operations but which are strangely devoid of even the most trivial details related to, for example, the murder of more than 30 000 Jews outside of Kiev by German units just a few days after its capture by the Germans. In fact, the histories from the 1950s and 1960s leave the impression that this was a war like any other.

Wehrmacht: The German armed forces, including the army, navy, and air force.

SS (Schutzstaffel): Literally, 'protective squad.' Led by Heinrich Himmler, the SS was responsible for administering and carrying out the Holocaust. A branch of the SS, the Waffen SS, served as combat units.

Over the last few decades new scholarship has emerged which makes these military histories not only perhaps superfluous but radically incomplete. It is now clear that the army was closely involved in implementing the Holocaust in the USSR and can in no way be considered to have waged a 'clean' war in the east (Wette, 2006). The war in the east and the Holocaust are so interconnected that they must be considered as a symbiotic whole, as flip sides to the same coin. 'Operation Barbarossa' can even be seen as the mechanism by which Hitler hoped to carry out his policy of gaining *lebensraum* while simultaneously engaging in ethnic cleansing (especially Slavs and Jews) in order to make room for German settlers. An examination of the planning for the invasion must therefore include planning for mass murder as well as operational planning.

Even before Hitler ordered the preparation of plans for the invasion of the Soviet Union, Halder held several meetings in order to assemble the information needed to plan such an invasion. On 26 July the head of army intelligence reported that the best chance of success for an invasion was 'in the direction of Moscow' with the ultimate intention of driving behind the Red Army and forcing it to fight with an inverted front (facing its rear). The key meeting took place on 31 July, when Hitler argued that Russia is a 'factor on which England is relying the most' and that 'Russia's destruction must therefore be made a part of this struggle' (Halder, 1988: 244). According to Halder's diary, Hitler made wide-ranging suggestions as to how the offensive would be conducted, including his belief that the attack could succeed only 'if [the] Russian state can be shattered to its roots with one blow.' He then laid out the plan of attack which would have brought Ukraine, Belorussia, and the Baltic states under German domination using 120 divisions in a double envelopment from the flanks (Halder, 1988: 245). This meeting was significant not only because it marks the 'turn to the east' but because Hitler presented his desires to the military leadership in terms of strategic necessity rather than ideological goals; his explicit goal was to deprive Britain of an ally and no mention was made of the ideological underpinnings. It is unclear if Hitler was simply tailoring his message to the particular audience (a favorite tactic of his when making speeches) or dissembling, but after this meeting the German high command began earnestly planning an invasion.

The plans went through several drafts, and the first one, prepared by Major-General **Erich Marcks** and completed on 5 August 1940, envisioned the primary objective, which remained the goal throughout all of the various plans, as the destruction of the Red Army west of the Dnepr River. This was to be achieved through massive encirclements which destroyed the Red Army and the ensuing pursuit of its remnants to a point from which they could no longer threaten German interests, in this case a line running from Rostov to Gorki and Archangel (approximately 1000 miles from the invasion

Marcks, Erich (1891–1944): General who wrote and submitted the first plan for 'Operation Barbarossa.' This plan formed the basis for subsequent plans and the final plan.

point). The major thrust was towards Moscow, with a subsidiary strike towards Kiev and a third, and much less important, strike towards Leningrad. The main effort was aimed at Moscow because Marcks assumed the Soviets would concentrate their forces to protect it, with the attack on Kiev coming after the capture of Moscow and the destruction of the last Soviet armies. After the three major cities had been captured it was assumed that all Soviet forces would be irredeemably disrupted and the army could then advance to its final line essentially unopposed. The entire invasion was envisioned as lasting about 9–17 weeks, depending upon weather and Soviet resistance. Marcks thought a German force of 147 infantry divisions, 24 panzer (tank), and 12 motorized infantry divisions was sufficient to defeat the Soviets, whom he believed had about 96 infantry divisions, 23 cavalry divisions, and 28 mechanized brigades.

The Supreme Command of the Army (OKH) developed a plan of its own which made the same basic assumptions as Marcks. It envisioned dividing its forces into three **Army Groups**: Army Group North aimed towards Leningrad; Army Group Center aimed at Smolensk and Moscow; and Army Group South aligned along an axis towards Kiev. The basic goal was still the destruction of the Red Army west of the Dnepr as close to the border as possible; the greatest fear was that the Red Army would retreat into the Soviet interior and thus escape destruction. Moscow remained a primary target since it was assumed the Soviets would concentrate their armies there to protect their capital, and Kiev and Leningrad remained important but secondary targets. Once these goals were achieved the army could push on to its final destination facing no coherent Soviet defense. The final goal was pushed several hundred miles beyond Marcks' goal to a line from Archangel to Astrakhan (the A–A line). The OKH thought the campaign would take 8–10 weeks; the force to accomplish this was envisioned as 105 infantry divisions and 32 armored and motorized divisions.

The plans were presented to Hitler at a meeting on 5 December 1940. He did not agree with either Marcks or OKH that Moscow should be a primary target; Leningrad was much more important both in prestige (it was the birthplace of Soviet communism) and economically (it was a major center of armament manufacturing), while the Ukraine possessed priceless agricultural and industrial products which would prove immediately useful both at the front and in Germany. His disagreement resulted, as usual with Hitler, not in the outright rejection of an attack upon Moscow but a failure to reach a clear decision about the main goal of the invasion. His ideas were crystalized in the final plan presented and signed on 18 December, with minor modifications at the last minute by Hitler [**Doc. 3, p. 111**]. The final plan envisioned an invasion along the three axes originally envisioned by Marcks: Leningrad, Smolensk–Moscow, and Kiev. The goal was to annihilate the Red

Army Group: An armed force composed of several armies, which were in turn formed from corps, which in turn were formed of several divisions. In German usage an army group usually comprised 3–4 armies. During the fighting on the Eastern Front the Germans divided their forces into three army groups: North, Center, and South (South was split and given other names at various times).

Army west of the Dvina–Dnepr rivers and to chase the survivors east of the A–A line. Moscow was not identified as a primary target but was left as a possible goal depending upon circumstances. The primary thrust would be in the center towards Smolensk with the goal of trapping and destroying the bulk of the Red Army, which the *Wehrmacht* believed was arrayed to protect the capital. Army Group Center was thus given the largest infantry, tank, and motorized forces so that it could accomplish the primary goal of 'Barbarossa:' the destruction of the Red Army. The Army Group was also to serve as a strategic reserve in that once it had destroyed the main Soviet forces it was to detach its armored units and send them to aid its northern and southern neighbors through **enveloping** pincer movements designed to clear those areas of surviving Red Army units. The plan had thus evolved from a relatively simple one of two main attacks (which nonetheless violated the military maxim of concentrating on a single goal) to one in which there were three main attacks with the possibility of at least three additional offensives if necessary. The final plan's diffuse goals and aims would be a major factor in its failure.

Envelop: In military usage, a maneuver which encircles an enemy formation. A single envelopment occurs when an enemy flank is penetrated to encircle the entire unit from one side; a double envelopment is when both flanks are penetrated and the unit is surrounded from both sides.

The discrepancy between the Marcks and OKH plans was the emphasis upon the importance of Moscow. On 5 December Hitler did not address this issue and so the final order laid the foundations for serious disagreements once operations commenced. The biggest problem for German strategy was that 'Barbarossa' set multiple and conflicting goals, including the military goal of destroying the Red Army, the economic goal of occupying as much of the Soviet Union as possible, and the political goal of destroying communism and creating the conditions for *lebensraum*. Hitler wore many hats and the order reflected his divergent priorities: he was at the same time political head of state, economic overlord, and supreme commander of the armed forces. But combined with the problem of diffuse goals was the failure of Hitler and the top military commanders to prepare contingency plans in case the Red Army did not collapse; this failure would become the single largest flaw of the entire operation. But whatever flaws existed within the plan, the Germans were certain they could win the war before they became critical, and do so within eight to ten weeks. A large reason behind the failure to create contingency plans was the low opinion many Germans had of Soviet inhabitants; Hitler believed, for example, that 'the Russian people are inferior. Their army is without leadership. Once the Russian army is beaten, then disaster cannot be forestalled.' (Halder, 1988: 297). A general echoed this sentiment when he stated that '[t]here will be fourteen days of heavy fighting. Hopefully, by then we shall have made it' (Förster, 1997: 129).

The hidden flaws within the plan included not just the neglect of contingency planning but the failure to address adequately the potential logistical problems. One of the key features of the war was the funnel shape of the

Eurasian landmass; this meant that the front line became increasingly longer the further the Germans advanced. The Germans realized they had insufficient forces to man effectively the A–A line and that supply lines would become increasingly tenuous the further east they advanced. On 22 June the front was about 800 miles from sea to sea, but by the time the Germans reached Moscow it would have nearly doubled to 1500 miles, and the A–A line was even further east and therefore longer. The most efficient method for moving to the A–A line in such a country would have been by rail, but the German railways were strained even before operations in the USSR began. There was a serious shortage of German rail cars as well as engines and in any event the Soviets used a wider gauge for their rail beds. This meant that railcars from western Europe could not be used until the system had been adapted, and in the meantime the army would have to rely upon captured Soviet rail stock. Even with the captured resources, however, it was unlikely that sufficient supplies could be brought forward; General **Friedrich Paulus** supervised a war game in December 1940 that showed logistical support for the invasion would break down even before the great battles of the Dnepr were completed and even if captured stock were utilized. This should have raised serious doubts about the operational plan, but as planning progressed the German high command acknowledged the problems but simply assumed that the war would be won by the time the lack of supplies became critical. Operational planning was thus marked by an irrational optimism that a quick victory would overcome any potential difficulties; as one recent scholar put it, reality was being adapted to the plan rather than vice-versa (Creveld, 2004).

Paulus, Friedrich (1890–1957): Commander of Sixth Army from January 1942, his task in 'Operation Blue' was to seize Stalingrad. Before the war he helped plan 'Operation Barbarossa.'

These transport deficiencies were duly noted by *Wehrmacht* commanders but were considered of little importance because the campaign was designed to achieve a rapid victory. For a quick campaign the German leadership, especially Hitler, envisioned motor vehicle transport (trucks) as more important than rails; the idea was to ship by rail as far east as possible and then to load all supplies into trucks for delivery to the front lines. The solution, as far as the German command was concerned, was thus not to solve logistical problems but to find the operational approach which permitted a victorious conclusion before logistical problems emerged. The problem with this approach, however, was that trucks require roads and these turned out to be scarce in the western Soviet Union in 1941 (especially paved roads). The further the Germans advanced the more precarious truck-based supply became, and once bad weather set in and turned the dirt roads into mud it became disastrous. By September 1941 a truck-based supply chain was clearly a serious mistake, and the transportation difficulties of the fall and early winter of 1941 were not caused by the winter or cold weather, but by a lack of planning (Schüler, 1997).

The army's economic plan for the utilization of the conquered regions suffered from its own flaws. General Georg Thomas was responsible for economic planning for the OKW and began preparing for the invasion during August 1940. Thomas concluded, based upon available information, that the invasion of the USSR would probably not provide much economic benefit to Germany because its economic surpluses (the amount above what the Soviet economy consumed) were not large enough to satisfy German demands. Thomas knew this was not what the command structures wanted to hear, however, and his final report of February 1941 claimed that Germany would acquire enough Soviet grain and industrial goods to satisfy all of its needs for at least two years. This legerdemain was accomplished by concluding that since 'the Russian is used to adjusting his consumption to bad harvests' all that was required was for the Germans to seize the majority of Soviet agricultural and industrial production; the Soviet people were, in other words, to be treated as if the crops had failed and starved in order to accomplish German economic goals. The 'hunger plan,' as it has been called, envisioned the seizure of all the grain normally exported from the Ukraine to the urban areas of the USSR and its shipment to Germany regardless of the fact that large population centers throughout the USSR would therefore face severe food shortages. German planners thus envisioned solving their supply problems by creating a major demographic crisis in Soviet cities. The resulting mass mortality would then decrease future Soviet food demands to a far lower and therefore sustainable level amid continuing exports to Germany. The deaths of millions of Soviet citizens would therefore create surplus foodstuffs for consumption in Germany. Thomas' report was ultimately used by Hitler as justification for the focus on the Ukrainian breadbasket rather than Moscow.

In addition to logistical and economic flaws, even German operational planning contained several serious shortcomings. No one in Germany possessed accurate figures for Soviet weapon or equipment production, the size or potential of the Red Army, or its disposition. The army staff responsible for collecting intelligence from the USSR, called Foreign Armies East (*FHO*), had no agents inside the Soviet Union and was unable to collect realistic data. It relied upon outdated information, guesswork, assumptions, and speculation. Even the state of the road network, which was the core of the logistical and operational plans, was unknown because the Germans lacked accurate and recent maps. The Germans could therefore make no definite conclusions as to what the Red Army was capable of, how it would react to the invasion, or even where its units were located. Even the requirement that the Red Army be destroyed west of the Dnepr and that it was concentrated in front of Moscow was based not upon knowledge of Soviet dispositions or strategy but upon German assumptions. The German intelligence staffs tried to provide their assumptions with a more solid foundation by relying upon known Soviet military performance, and the war with Finland during the winter of 1939–40 was seen as a key indicator of Soviet potential (the impressive Soviet victory over Japan during the spring of 1939 was, however, ignored). German intelligence agencies also placed a great deal of emphasis upon the purges of the army during the late 1930s. But these provided poor guidance as to how the Red Army would function once hostilities began. The Red Army had indeed performed poorly during its war with Finland, especially in its handling of armor and artillery units. It suffered grievous casualties as it failed to maneuver properly and supply its troops, and its failure to manage properly the battlefield was obvious to the intelligence services of the *Wehrmacht*. But the Germans missed the reforms initiated in the wake of this disaster and failed to appreciate that by March 1940 the Soviets had begun to overcome organizational difficulties.

The military purges, which began in 1937, were thought to have had a serious impact upon the Soviet armed forces. Of five marshals of the Soviet Union only two were not executed, of 30 army commanders only one survived, and of 85 members of the council for defense 72 were either shot, died in prison or committed suicide. It is now generally recognized that around 75 per cent of the top commanders of the Red army were purged during this period, including 231 of 287 divisional commanders (Bonwetsch, 1997: 396–7). As the terror spiraled downwards into lower ranks it created an atmosphere in which initiative and independence of thought were thoroughly squashed. However, the purge did not, contrary to the assumptions of the Germans, destroy the fighting power of the Red Army. It made the process of creating a modern fighting force more difficult, to be sure, but it did not leave the USSR with an army devoid of an effective leadership (Reese, 1996). The problem for German intelligence services was that they missed this key fact and assumed that the Red Army was, as Hitler put it, 'leaderless.'

The intelligence flaws fostered an assessment, shared by all levels of the German command from Hitler downwards, which predicted a rapid German victory before the Soviets could utilize the vast resources of the Soviet Union. The key to victory was not to solve the economic or logistical problems the invasion engendered, but to create an operational plan which could accomplish victory before these became serious handicaps. The intelligence failures were thus combined with a planning system whose emphasis was upon operations rather than solving problems. The primacy of operations meant that military operations were planned before anything else; the logistics plan, formulated after the operational goals had been set, had the task of finding a way to accomplish the operational plan regardless of difficulties. This meant that any supply difficulties were secondary to operations and did not impact the plan's chances for implementation; for example, the plain fact that supplies of rubber tires for trucks would run out in July 1941 was a serious threat to operations, so the solution was not to find more tires but to devise an operations plan which guaranteed victory before the supply of tires was exhausted.

The final plan, code named 'Operation Barbarossa,' envisioned three army groups (North, Center, and South) totaling 152 divisions (19 tank divisions and 15 motorized) of about 3 500 000 men, 3350 tanks, and 2770 aircraft under the overall command of OKH. Added to these powerful forces were several Finnish and Romanian divisions. Army Group North, under the command of Field Marshal **Wilhelm von Leeb**, was to strike north through the Baltic states towards Leningrad, its ultimate goal. To accomplish this it was given 18 divisions organized into two armies (Sixteenth and Eighteenth Armies) as well as three panzer and two motorized divisions (organized into *Panzergruppe* 4). It had reserves of two motorized divisions and an SS division. Army Group Center, under Field Marshal **Fedor von Bock**, was given two of the four armored groups (*Panzergruppe* 2 and *Panzergruppe* 3), consisting of nine panzer, one cavalry, six motorized, and 11 infantry divisions, as well as 20 infantry divisions organized into two armies (Ninth and Fourth). It was to strike northeastward towards Smolensk and Moscow. Army Group South, under Field Marshal Gerd von Rundstedt, consisted of *Panzergruppe* 1 (four panzer and seven motorized divisions), and 22 infantry divisions in three armies (Sixth, Eleventh, and Seventeenth). It had seven infantry and a panzer division in reserve and was to strike towards Kiev. The overall goal of all the army groups was to trap and destroy the Red Army as close to the border as possible and prevent it from retreating to the east where it would have posed a serious threat.

While the traditional view of the *Wehrmacht* is that it was a technological marvel in 1941, in reality most of its forces remained no more mobile than its predecessors during the First World War. In addition to the 600 000 motor vehicles there were 625 000 horses, most of them draught animals for hauling artillery or supplies (most of the heavy equipment was still horse-drawn); only the motorized divisions used motor vehicles to move men, equipment, and supplies. The rest of the troops had to march and bring both supplies and artillery up by horses and the German army was, in 1941, still an old-fashioned army which moved by either human or animal power (Bartov, 1992).

'Operation Barbarossa' was not merely a military operation. It also had political and racial goals and these required thorough planning as well. The people and institutions responsible for this aspect included Hitler, the army and its leadership, and the SS and its leadership. On 30 March 1941 Hitler made a speech to the top commanders of the *Wehrmacht* during which he claimed that this was to be a war of extermination unlike any other war, and

Leeb, Wilhelm von (1876 −1956): Commander of Army Group North from June 1941–January 1942, when he was retired.

Bock, Fedor von (1880– 1945): Commander of Army Group Center from June 1941 until December 1941. In January 1942 he was given command of Army Group South for 'Operation Blue' until disagreements with Hitler led to his retirement in July 1942. Died when his car was strafed in May, 1945.

that communists were criminals who deserved no quarter. The usual rules of engagement, where civilians were to be treated with respect and measures were taken to avoid harming them, were to be jettisoned in favor of the radical conception of viewing all Soviet citizens as either actual or potential enemies. It was, he claimed, a race war where the usual tender mercies towards non-combatants would be discarded. The only way to ensure that potential enemies did not become actual enemies was utter ruthlessness.

The security of the rear areas thus assumed a heightened importance, and the earliest document related to this aspect of the war was issued by OKW on 13 March 1941 [**Doc. 4, p. 112**]. It specified that **Heinrich Himmler** and the *SS* had been assigned 'special tasks' by Hitler and that he was therefore empowered to carry these out on his own authority and without interference from the *Wehrmacht*. In order to clarify how this would function in the field, **Reinhard Heydrich** (head of the SS Main Office for Reich Security) and General Eduard Wagner, responsible for army rear area security, negotiated a delineation of tasks for areas behind the front lines on 26 March. The order which resulted from these negotiations, signed by the head of the army on 28 April, permitted 'special detachments' (**Einsatzgruppen**) of the *SS* to carry out the 'special tasks' given to Himmler. These units, hand-picked by Heydrich himself, were to ensure political security in German-occupied areas by arresting and 'handling' people perceived as possible enemies. Himmler issued further orders which gave his units responsibility for all security behind the front lines, a task which the army was very pleased to pass on because this freed it from having to do the job itself.

The *Einsatzgruppen* consisted of four units totaling about 3000 men. They were assigned to newly conquered areas behind the army groups and were responsible for the security of rear echelon military units. Each *gruppe* was subdivided into *kommandos* which operated separately and independently so that they could cover larger areas at the same time. The men had been selected by Heydrich from police units and various *SS* organizations (one of Himmler's many jobs included that of chief of all German police), and he was careful to choose men who could be trusted to carry out their 'special tasks.' At a meeting sometime during the spring or summer of 1941, Heydrich or his deputy gave the commanders of three of the *gruppen* their general instructions, which included a detailed list of the people to be arrested (communist functionaries, Jews in the Communist party, and anyone committing sabotage) as well as general instructions on how to deal with them. An order on 29 June on 'self-cleansing campaigns' from Heydrich instructed the commanders to encourage surreptitiously local anti-Semites to initiate pogroms which were expected to spin out of control. In this way anti-Semitic 'actions' could not be blamed entirely upon the Germans and locals could be integrated into the activities of the *gruppen*. These orders laid the foundations for

Himmler, Heinrich (1900–1945): Head of the *SS* and chief of all German police. He was responsible for operating the concentration and death camps as well as directing the *Einsatzgruppen*.

Heydrich, Reinhard (1904–42): Chief of domestic security, responsible for creating the mechanisms of the Holocaust, including the *Einsatzgruppen*, which he created and which reported to him. Assassinated by Czech agents.

Einsatzgruppen: Four mobile murder squads of approximately 500–1000 men each organized by Reinhard Heydrich. Their task was to round up and shoot communists, Jews, and anyone politically suspect behind the front lines. They were responsible for up to 1.5 million deaths on the eastern front.

the subsequent murders of between 500 000 and 1 500 000 Jews in the USSR (Longerich, 1997).

But it was not only the *SS* which was permitted wide latitudes in its behavior towards Soviet citizens. Every army has rules and laws which govern how its soldiers can interact and treat civilians in combat zones as well as in the rear areas behind the front lines. Actions committed against civilians which would be considered crimes in civil law, such as rape, burglary, or murder, are considered crimes by military codes and the offender is punished accordingly. But Hitler and the military command did not wish to see Germans punished for waging racial war against an 'inferior' enemy. Accordingly, an army order of 13 May [**Doc. 5, p. 113**] absolved all German soldiers of guilt from anything they did which normally fell under the army's criminal code; by freeing soldiers from legal responsibility for their actions against civilians this order gave free rein to the troops to kill anyone, civilian or military, suspected of being, for whatever reason, hostile and dangerous. The types of people considered 'hostile' were spelled out in an order on 19 May which warned the troops to pay special attention to all Bolsheviks, saboteurs, and Jews. But perhaps the most cynical and inhuman of documents issued before the war was the 'Guidelines for the Treatment of Political Commissars,' issued on 6 June 1941 [**Doc. 6, p. 113**]. It ordered the immediate separation and murder of anyone who was a political officer in the Red Army, a violation of the Geneva Convention and of basic military law, both of which provide protection to all unarmed soldiers captured during operations. As part of this racial war in the east, Germans soldiers were being ordered to commit murder.

But not only political prisoners were to be murdered; even ordinary prisoners were not to be treated with kindness. The orders regarding the treatment of prisoners of war were issued 16 June. They began with the usual injunction that this was a life and death struggle between Bolshevism and Germany and that any resistance by prisoners, no matter how slight, was to be crushed with the utmost violence. It also pointed out that the USSR had not signed the Geneva Convention of 1929 (which was true) and that therefore its regulations did not apply to captured Soviet prisoners (which was not true because signatories, like Germany, were enjoined to provide the protections to all nations). The names of Soviet prisoners would therefore not be registered with the Red Cross and, more ominously, they would be required to perform menial tasks for the army (such as digging defensive barriers). Finally, it was ordered that all prisoners be congregated in locations sufficiently far enough behind the lines to pose no threat to operations. Roughly 5 700 000 Soviet soldiers were captured by the Germans during the war, mostly during 1941–42. Of these it is estimated that 3 300 000, or 57.5 per cent, died in German captivity, mostly from neglect and disease (in comparison, the death rate among British and American prisoners of the Germans was 3.5 per cent of the total). Most of these unfortunate men, 2 000 000 of them, were already dead by February 1942, eight months after the war began (Streit, 2004). German regulations for Soviet POWs resulted in their almost total neglect by their German captors and their subsequent deaths in vast numbers. In Sixth Army of Army Group South there was a standing order, for example, that any POW who failed to obey all orders was to be shot immediately. Reich Marshal **Hermann Göring** summed up German attitudes towards the hundreds of thousands of men in German POW camps by decreeing on 16 September that Germany was not, in fact, obligated to feed these men but would do so based upon their ability to contribute to the German war effort through forced labor. This was, of course, a death sentence to those too sick or injured to work, or to anyone who refused to contribute to the German war effort through their labor.

The Germans simply failed to prepare for the huge numbers of prisoners they took, which is a significant oversight given that the operational plan envisioned the collapse of the Red Army west of the Dnepr. It was not until October 1941 that the Germans began to realize better management of their prisoners was necessary, and even then they decided to take care only of those prisoners able and willing to work. This resulted in a slow decline in the number of Soviet prisoners who died in German custody, but nonetheless large numbers continued to die until the very end of the war.

Göring, Hermann (1893 –1946): Commander of the *Luftwaffe*, economic czar of Germany, and the designated successor to Hitler until April 1945.

SOVIET PREPARATIONS FOR WAR

Front: In Soviet usage, a front was a group of armies (of various sizes) led and directed by a common headquarters and was roughly analogous to a German army group but much smaller. These were continually renamed and were called, for example, West Front, Stalingrad Front, etc. After the Red Army began liberating Soviet territory from the Germans they were numbered and given regional names, for example, First Belorussian Front. In general terms a front is the area at which fighting occurs between enemies.

During peacetime the Red Army divided the entire country into military districts. During hostilities these were transformed into *fronts*, which were somewhat similar to the German army groups but slightly smaller and with greater responsibilities, including training, mobilization, and all military activities within their boundaries. In 1941 there were 16 military districts in the USSR and one *front*, in the far east facing Japan. This system, in theory, permitted the rapid creation of command staffs capable of immediately resisting an invasion.

The 1938 Universal Military Service Law made all Soviet men up to age 50 liable for basic military training. By 1941 the USSR had a pool of about 14 million such reservists, which was unknown to German intelligence and planners. As entire armies were ground up by the German advance, this law permitted the Soviets to bring up vast numbers of replacements, an event unforeseen by the Germans and something they could not themselves have accomplished.

During the period between the pact in 1939 and the invasion in 1941 the leadership of the Soviet Union and its Red Army knew that dangers lurked outside its borders. During the 1930s the USSR had spent a great deal of time and effort constructing formidable defensive works along its European border. The Nazi–Soviet pact and the border readjustments which followed the dismemberment of Poland made it necessary to move the Red Army (and the military districts) several hundred kilometers westward, making these extensive defensive fortifications useless. Most of these fortifications were hurriedly dismantled, transported, and reconstructed in new positions, but when the Germans invaded almost none of them had been completely reinstalled. In June 1941 the Red Army was still in the process of organizing defensive works and implementing its defensive doctrine and was therefore unprepared for defensive warfare.

Soviet defensive theory refused to permit war to be fought on Soviet territory and envisioned war as primarily offensive. The Red Army was to halt an invader at the border and then launch strategic counterstrikes designed to take the war into enemy territory. Under Marshal **Semyon Timoshenko** the Soviets developed a series of war plans in 1940–41, each emphasizing offensive rather than defensive strategies. The plans highlighted the intention to launch a major counter-offensive into enemy positions early into a German invasion in order to both disrupt the enemy offensive and take the war into German territory. Since the counterattack was to come early, the available forces had to be placed relatively close to the frontier and be at a high state of readiness. The air bases similarly had to be as close to the frontier as possible so that they could arrive and participate in the battle at the borders. Soviet planners expected the Germans to try to wrest control of the Ukraine's vast agricultural and industrial produce early in an invasion and therefore expected the main German effort to be south of the Pripet marshes into the Ukraine. In order to stop such an incursion and to have forces available for a counterstrike the Red Army concentrated large forces, especially armored units, in the Kiev Military District. The concentration of powerful forces in this sector would also, it was thought, provide the best avenue for conducting strategic operations against German forces elsewhere and destroying their fighting capabilities.

The defensive plan which the Soviets eventually adopted, called Mobilization Plan 41, called for over 200 divisions in three belts controlled by five *fronts*: North (formed from the Leningrad Military District); Northwestern (formed from the Baltic Special Military District); Western and Southwestern (which split the Western Special and Kiev Special Districts between them); and Southern (formed from the Odessa Military District). These would in turn be controlled by a Supreme High Command (*Stavka*), based in Moscow. The main task of the frontier forces was to slow down the

Timoshenko, Semyon (1895–1970): Held high ranking positions with the Red Army at various times, including *Front* commander during most of the major battles on the Eastern Front.

Stavka: The overall command of the Red Army. Its head was Stalin, and it consisted of various men over time, all top-ranking generals. Its members were often sent on missions to various fronts facing crises. Zhukov and Vasilevsky were Stavka representatives at various points of the war.

enemy so that the two belts further east, where the main striking force was located, could mobilize and then launch devastating offensives into the enemy's homeland. In June 1941 the first echelon had about 171 infantry divisions and 20 mechanized corps, while the second had about 57 infantry divisions (the third echelon had not yet been mobilized).

In June 1941 the Red Army had about 2 500 000 men on its western borders. It had about 20 000 tanks, but of these only 1225 were the modern T-34 and another 640 were the super-heavy tanks known as KV-1 and KV-2, while the rest were much smaller and essentially obsolete. It is important to keep in mind, however, that Soviet tanks were not necessarily inferior to German tanks, as tank standards in 1941 were not very high. Most German tanks were lightly armed and armored, just like most Soviet models. The one major advantage all German tanks possessed was that each of them had radio communications with the others in their unit. Only Soviet tank unit commanders had radios, which meant that their tanks operated singly on the battlefield rather than as teams. This was a significant drawback which would take time and experience to correct.

The Red Army in 1941 has been described as a 'blunt instrument.' The essential problem was that the USSR was still a peasant society in the process of modernization. The rapid industrialization which had marked the Soviet economy during the 1930s had its counterpart in the army: the technology, materiel, and modern weapons were being produced but the ability to use these effectively developed much more slowly (Reese, 1996). The purges of the 1930s hampered the army's ability to adapt to such radical change, but was less critical in blunting its effectiveness than rapid expansion and modernization (Reese, 1996). The real effect of the purges was to sap the confidence of the commanders during the first months of the war as they feared the personal consequences of their potential mistakes. This fear did not begin to abate until October 1942 with the launching of operations against Army Group South (Bonwetsch, 1997). The problem was not that the Germans were superior soldiers or that the USSR suffered under a tyrannical dictator (as did the Germans), but that the technological knowledge necessary for a modern army did not yet exist among the members of the mass Red Army. Officers, for example, were often unable to coordinate or effectively use the weapons and formations entrusted to them because they had not been trained properly in their use. In 1941 the USSR possessed weapons at least as effective, and in some cases superior, to those of the Germans, but did not possess the skill or training to use them properly. The units were also not up to strength, had not been adequately trained, and were simply not ready for the kind of mobile modern warfare practiced by the Germans (Glantz and House, 1995). The first year of the war gave the Red Army this experience and permitted it to 'learn to fight' over the course of 1942–43

(Reese, 1996). Even the German general **Heinz Guderian**, who fought through many of the battles on the Eastern Front, said after the war that 'nothing would be worse than to underrate the strength of a great nation as full of life as the Russian' (Liddell Hart, 1956: 133). The Red Army was a giant capable of great deeds, but at the same time it was less capable than it should have been.

Guderian, Heinz (1888–1954): One of the foremost Panzer specialists, Guderian commanded Second Panzer group of Army Group Center during 1941. His disagreements with Hitler led to his retirement in December 1941, but after the debacle at Stalingrad he was recalled as inspector of Panzer Troops. In July 1944 he was made Chief of the General Staff, but was dismissed after arguments with Hitler in March 1945.

2

22 June 1941: The Invasion

THE BORDER BATTLES

2 1 June 1941 was a Saturday. Late that afternoon the codeword 'Dortmund' was sent out from OKH to the German command posts along the eastern border with the USSR; the invasion would go ahead as planned early the next morning. The first German units across the border on 22 June were special forces whose job was to cut communication and electrical power networks. This was particularly important because the Soviets mistrusted wireless communications and relied upon telephones, telegraphs, and wired radio networks for communications between headquarters and their subordinate units. Severing communications between Soviet military units was one of the most important tasks and had to be accomplished as early as possible in order to cause the greatest possible confusion among the Red Army. Special forces were also required to seize as many bridges as possible so that tanks and infantry could quickly cross into Soviet territory to begin their missions.

In response to the invasion the Soviets formed on 23 June the General Supreme Headquarters (*Stavka*), with Stalin, **Kliment Voroshilov**, **Nikolai Kuznetsov**, Semyon Timoshenko (the titular head of *Stavka*, but in fact real authority lay with Stalin), **Vyacheslav Molotov**, Semyon Budenny, and **Georgii Zhukov**. Overall command of all Soviet military assets lay with this committee, including those at the front as well as those being organized on the home front. On 24 June another of the most important decisions of the war was made in the Kremlin. A committee was created and given the task of relocating vital war industries to the east of the Ural mountains. By the end of 1941 over 2500 industrial factories had been relocated from the threatened western areas to the east, including almost 700 to the far reaches of Siberia. Included in the shipments were the archives of various governmental agencies, the convertible hard currencies of the Kremlin Armory (gold, diamonds, platinum), and even Lenin's body. These relocations were vital to

Voroshilov, Kliment (1881–1969): Red Army general, minister of defense before the war, and a member of the GKO.

Kuznetsov, Nikolai (1904–74): Commander of the Red Navy during the war, he was part of the highest leadership circles during the war.

Molotov, Vyacheslav (1890–1986): Soviet minister for foreign affairs, he and Ribbentrop negotiated the Nazi–Soviet Pact of 1939.

Zhukov, Georgii (1896–1974): Deputy Supreme Commander of the Red Army, Zhukov was instrumental in most of the major Soviet operations during the war, including the defense of Moscow, Stalingrad, Leningrad, Kursk, the operations in 1944, and the assault on Berlin.

maintaining production from factories whose original locations were overrun by the Germans and was one of the most well organized and successful logistical accomplishments of the war (Bellamy, 2007).

The primary task of the German army groups was to destroy all Soviet units as far west as possible and thus destroy the Soviet ability to resist a breakout of German units into the interior of the USSR. This goal was somewhat similar to what had happened in France: once the bulk of the enemy army had been destroyed in vast encirclements (such as at Dunkirk) the rest could be pursued and easily destroyed. The entrapment and destruction of the Red Army west of the Dnepr–Dvina line would not only prevent a massive retreat into the Russian interior but would then leave the areas east of that line ripe for occupation by the Germans.

The opening salvos of the war were not only artillery shells but bombs dropped by the German air force, the **Luftwaffe**. It was given the task of destroying targets on the ground, including not only enemy aircraft but bridges, columns of enemy troops, and vehicles. There were so many targets that the *Luftwaffe* became, in many ways, an adjunct of the army as it flew missions in support of ground objectives. But the air force was not originally intended to serve as close ground support, and a robust German presence in the air was the manifestation not necessarily of German air superiority (to some extent it was indicative of German control of the skies), but also of the problems experienced by the troops; when neither artillery nor tanks could deal with enemy formations (especially if these included the T-34 or KV tanks) the air force was called in to break them up. The use of the air force as ground support thus reflected the army's lack of heavy artillery rather than a doctrine of close ground support.

Just as important as close ground support during the opening hours were the successes against the Red Air Force. The *Luftwaffe's* major targets during the first days were Soviet air bases and the Germans made every effort to destroy enemy planes on the ground so as not to have to face them in the air or permit them to interfere with German ground operations. During the first 24 hours approximately 800 Soviet aircraft were destroyed on the ground and another 200 were shot down in aerial combat; this was a serious loss for an air force which possessed around 7500 aircraft. The Germans continued to bomb Soviet air bases, which were close to the front, and engage in dogfights over the battlefield during the initial part of the campaign and crippled the ability of the Red Air Force to either counterattack or provide close ground support to its own troops.

The successes in the air were echoed by successes on land. Despite stout resistance on the part of some Soviet units, German forces crossed the borders everywhere, mostly on bridges since the Soviets were able to destroy very few of the river crossings. The invasion caught Soviet forces completely

Luftwaffe: The German air force, headed by Hermann Göring. It played a large role during the early days of the war but was gradually pushed from the skies.

unprepared and the Germans used this element of surprise to their advantage. The German ability to mobilize millions of men and thousands of vehicles along the border without being discovered by Soviet intelligence is one of the greatest enigmas of the war. It seemed as if the Soviets had closed their eyes to all the ominous signs of impending invasion and simply ignored all the warning signs. We now know that the Soviet intelligence agencies knew about German preparations and had received multiple warnings from trustworthy sources, including foreign leaders and German deserters. Stalin mistrusted this intelligence as disinformation planted by German spies and had some of the messengers shot (including at least one German deserter). But even the warnings passed along by Churchill were ignored by Stalin because he thought it was an attempt to provoke the Soviets into military action which would spark war with Germany. Following Stalin's lead, the main Soviet intelligence agency branded most of the warnings from Britain and the United States as disinformation planted by German spies. Stalin was apparently convinced that Hitler would never attack the USSR as long as he was at war with Britain, and Soviet intelligence services merely confirmed his interpretation of foreign intelligence; any information to the contrary was ignored while the messengers were punished (Murphy, 2005). During the first hours of the invasion, Stalin's disbelief even caused him to question whether the invasion was a provocation by German generals acting independently of Hitler, and the Soviet commanders of frontier units were ordered not to return fire without first seeking approval. The units facing the brunt of the invasion thus found themselves under incredible pressure from both the enemy and their own commanders. One flustered unit signaled to its commander that it was under fire and requested instructions, to which he replied 'You must be mad. And why wasn't your signal in code?' The result of Stalin's belief that Hitler would never attack complicated efforts to resist the invasion and precious time and resources were lost as confusion and shock crippled the frontier units and the high command. The Germans also exploited this confusion to their advantage.

The first major objective of Army Group Center was the fortress at the city of Brest-Litovsk, which sits at the border on the river Bug. The German 45th Infantry Division launched a heavy artillery barrage against the city but failed to dislodge the defenders, about 3500 men. The Germans continued hammering the fortress as panzers raced eastward, isolating and surrounding it. The last defenders did not cease fighting until 20 July, or almost a month after the invasion, although the Germans classified it as captured on 30 June when organized resistance collapsed. The fierce fighting at Brest, which ranged from heavy artillery to hand-to-hand fighting, is a good indicator of the resistance of scattered Soviet units in the face of overwhelming German forces during the first days. While many Soviet units simply collapsed in the face of the onslaught, many followed the example of those at Brest; one German commander reported, for example, that a single KV-1 tank held up his entire division for two days because it blocked the only road. Several German tanks had fired upon the monster but their shells simply bounced off the KV's thickly armored hull. After serious losses and the loss of valuable time, an anti-aircraft gun, the powerful 88 mm, was brought up and finally destroyed the Soviet tank. Along the Nieman river the German tanks encountered the Soviet T-34, arguably the best tank of any belligerent of the entire war. The Soviets had destroyed a German tank leading a column across a bridge and thus blocked all traffic. About 30 German tanks opened fire on the T-34s but their shells bounced off the thick and sharply angled armor which the T-34 possessed on its front edges. The German anti-tank weapons were of no help, as their shells simply bounced off the T-34s as well. The Germans cleared the bridge and the area of enemy tanks only when another 88 mm anti-aircraft gun was put to work and the Soviets were driven off. These examples may have been relatively isolated ones, but they surprised and shocked the Germans who experienced them.

Brest was one objective of Army Group Center, but its main goal was to destroy the Red Army. This was to be accomplished through pincers on either flank of the Soviet *Front* which were to slam shut behind it and trap its entire force. There were only two real roads in the region of the army group's advance, one heading eastward from Brest and another leading to Minsk. Guderian, who was in command of the panzer units facing Brest and whose forces formed one of the pincers, went to the banks of the Bug to examine his crossing points and saw that the Soviets were not manning defensive points opposite his position. His tanks promptly crossed the river and proceeded to drive eastward at a high rate, followed by Guderian himself, who crossed the river just three and one-half hours after the first of his tanks. Guderian's unit consisted of 27 000 vehicles and 60 000 men, and the traffic across the river was so immense that he personally organized the crossings so that the panzers could advance quickly. The main crossing area of Army Group Center's armor on the Bug was not fully clear until 26 June, but the bulk of Guderian's armor made it across by 23 June. Their goal was to move as fast as possible to link up with General **Hermann Hoth's** Third Panzer Group on the northern flank of the army group and thus close the pincers around Special Western District.

In the operational area of Army Group Center, the end of the first day saw two entire Soviet *fronts*, Northwestern and the Western, driven back from the border and largely shattered. The lack of communication, surprise, and inertia of Soviet units deprived the *fronts* of their ability to resist effectively the German invasion. It proved impossible for General **Dmitry Pavlov** and his *front* commanders to know what was going on and to create viable and

Hoth, Hermann (1885 –1971): Commander of a panzer group during the early part of 'Barbarossa,' by 1942 he was the army commander who lost the second battle for Kharkov. He participated in 'Operation Blue' as a panzer army commander and led the attempt to relieve Stalingrad after it was surrounded. During the late summer of 1943 he was blamed for the spectacular advance of the Red Army in the Ukraine and fired by Hitler. He remained sidelined until the last weeks of the war.

Pavlov, Dmitry (1897– 1941): Red Army general and commander of West Front during the invasion in June, 1941. He bore the blame for his front's collapse and was shot.

realistic countermeasures. The Soviet units at the frontier had no knowledge of what was happening beyond what they could physically see of the battle-field, no orders from Pavlov, and this chaos made it nearly impossible for them to offer any kind of effective resistance to the German onslaught. For example, the attack deprived the headquarters of the Soviet Fourth Army, part of Pavlov's command in Minsk, of contact with both Pavlov and its own divisions. The commander of Fourth Army had no idea what was happening anywhere along his own *front*, let alone on neighboring sectors. Third and Tenth armies also had trouble maintaining contact with their units on the front lines. Pavlov thus had little idea what was going on at the front and could not report to his superiors in Moscow whether his troops were advancing, holding, or retreating. As a last resort his deputy flew to Tenth Army headquarters late on 22 June to ascertain the circumstances and order an immediate counterattack into German lines. He found, much to his surprise, a shattered army incapable of holding its own positions and in no position to attack. Pavlov's command was literally falling to pieces in the face of the invasion and there was little he could do to stem the collapse or gain the initiative.

Third Panzer Group, under Hoth, had meanwhile shoved its way into the gap between Western and Northwestern *Fronts* and was racing towards Vilnius, more than 100 miles behind the front lines. The Soviets ordered a massive armored strike against Third Panzer's right flank but, by the time it was organized and launched, Hoth's panzers had already reached Vilnius. Second Panzer Group, under Guderian, had pushed past Soviet units on the southern part of the front and was now trying, in conjunction with Hoth's panzers, to envelop Minsk and encircle the entire *front*. The battle for Minsk began on 26 June, a mere four days after the invasion. Pavlov, in anticipation of losing the city, had moved his headquarters to Mogilev earlier that day. Hoth's panzer group was 18 miles north of the city as Guderian closed in on it from the east. The two tank commanders pushed their troops as hard as possible in order to close the pocket tightly and prevent a breakout by the surrounded Soviet troops. On 28 June the armored pincers met at Minsk and loosely closed two pockets around Bialystok and another west of Minsk, and in the process captured almost the entire Soviet force facing Army Group Center. On 29 June the pincers around Bialystok were firmly closed, trapping 290 000 prisoners. Pavlov's forces had been crushed.

The capture of Minsk, the capital of the Belorussian Soviet republic, caused panic in Moscow among the top commanders. Nikita Khrushchev, who was the political commissar for the Ukraine when the war began, said after the war that Stalin suffered a breakdown when the Germans invaded that lasted until his speech on 3 July. During this time he was incapacitated from his anguish over the turn of events. It is now clear that nothing of the sort happened and that Stalin in fact kept up a rigorous schedule of crucial meetings at the Kremlin during that first week. He was shaken by the fall of Minsk on 28 June, but even then kept fully in touch with events until the next day, when he left the Kremlin for the first time since 22 June for his summer home outside Moscow. On 30 June a delegation from the government arrived there to tell him he had been chosen to lead the State Committee of Defense (**GKO**), which had been given complete control over all aspects of the economy, government, military, and in fact all aspects of Soviet life. Stalin, who seemed 'worried' according to one of the witnesses, asked 'Why have you come?' It may be that Stalin expected a coup against him, for when told why they came he seemed 'astonished.' Stalin, as head of the GKO and *Stavka*, then got back to work at the Kremlin (Bellamy, 2007: 221–8).

> **GKO:** Soviet State Committee of Defense, organized on 30 June and given broad nearly dictatorial powers over the USSR. It ran the war and country until 4 September 1945, two days after Japan surrendered.

One of the most important speeches Stalin ever made was broadcast to the entire Soviet Union on 3 July [**Doc. 7, p. 114**]. This speech is remarkable for several reasons, among them that he addressed the people as 'brothers and sisters' and emphasized Russian patriotism by referring to the invasion as an attack on the 'motherland.' Stalin pulled few punches in this speech and discussed the serious bombing of several large cities and the loss of significant territory along the western border. He said that the German goal was to destroy the freedoms and 'national existence' of the Soviet peoples and that the choice facing the USSR was either to remain free or 'fall into slavery.' This was a tough and cruel war between peoples in which there could be 'no mercy to the enemy.' He ordered the creation, in areas already occupied and by remnants of Soviet units, of guerilla forces whose job was to destroy the German communications and supply networks. An unintended consequence of this part of the speech was that the Germans now felt that their rear areas were threatened by partisans and began enacting draconian measures against perceived acts of aggression by Soviet civilians. An order of 23 July [**Doc. 8, p. 115**] ordered that civilian attacks could be contained only by the 'spreading of such terror' that few would be brave enough to act, and that the security forces should enact 'draconian measures' to ensure no further attacks occurred. This was license to murder soldiers, civilians, and anyone perceived as 'resisting' the Germans. But no one recognized this aspect of the speech and it was well received among the Soviet population, which felt relieved that Stalin had spoken about the war and promised victory.

Stavka's main order of business during the early days was to restore the situation in the center. Timoshenko was immediately sent to replace Pavlov, who was arrested and, after a trial that lasted about three weeks, shot along with his senior officers for cowardice. On 30 June **Andrei Yeremenko** took over Western *Front* from Timoshenko, but by this time all effective Soviet resistance west of the Dnepr in the central sector had collapsed. By 3 July German confidence was so high that Halder wrote in his diary that the goals

> **Yeremenko, Andrei** (1892–1970): *Front* commander who participated in most of the major operations of the Eastern Front.

of destroying the Red Army had already been accomplished and that the war had been won 'in the space of a few weeks' [**Doc. 9, p. 115**].

Bock, realizing the collapse of Soviet resistance meant that a larger encirclement was within reach, suggested that the panzers should continue eastward and close the pocket at Smolensk instead of Minsk, but Hitler was afraid this would put the German advance units at risk of being cut off from the infantry and ordered the panzers to meet at Minsk. This **cauldron** developed into a 'floating pocket' moving slowly eastward as Soviet units tried to escape. The few escaping Soviet forces could, and did, pose difficulties for the rear of German units; for example Second Panzer found that encircled Red Army units cut its supply lines to the west. The pocket therefore took longer than expected to clear, but the infantry slowly caught up and sealed the pocket, allowing the tanks to proceed to the next mission. The Minsk pocket was finally cleared on 16 July of 310 000 prisoners. Between the Bialystok and Minsk pockets over 600 000 Red Army prisoners were captured.

Closing and sealing the pockets around Bialystok and Minsk had proven more difficult than the German commanders had hoped, mostly because the tanks had advanced so far ahead of the accompanying infantry that the gap between them grew too large to prevent Soviet units from escaping the traps. The bulk of the tanks, far ahead of the infantry, found themselves placed in the role of fighting fleeing Soviets rather than driving eastward; the combat principle was that tanks did not stand and fight but drove quickly through enemy lines while the infantry stayed behind to do the bulk of the fighting. But at Bialystok and Minsk the tanks had to fulfill the role of infantrymen because the foot soldiers were simply too far behind. The pace of operations thus slowed as some tank units, the spearheads of the invasion, remained immobile for a week while they tried to create a firm seal around the eastern edge of the pockets. The pocket battles were a disaster for the Red Army, but the excess time they absorbed was problematic for the *Wehrmacht* as the commanders knew that the lost time was not to their benefit since they needed and had planned a quick victory. The German timetable was thus being put off schedule during the first days of battle not by Soviet resistance (which was effective in only a few areas) but, ironically, by success.

While Timoshenko was in command of Western *Front* he had tried to create a viable front to stop the Germans from thrusting eastward. He knew an attack would have to come through the Vitebsk area and organized a fairly robust resistance in the region. But parts of Second Panzer were already on the Dnepr at Rogachev while another part was already at Borisov on the Berezina; these were much further east than some of Timoshenko's own units. On 3 July the two panzer groups were merged into one and given the task of crossing the Dnepr and pushing as hard as possible towards Yelnia

Cauldron: When a military unit is surrounded and behind enemy lines it is said to be captured in a 'cauldron.' Many of the battles of the Eastern Front were cauldron battles.

and Smolensk to complete the capture of the vital Orsha–Vitebsk area. Bock ordered Second Panzer to attack southward towards Mogilev and Borisov while Third Panzer was to take Vitebsk, in the north. By 11 July both armored groups had reached their goals and began to execute a double envelopment of Smolensk. The encirclement began with the northern armored pincer moving forward from Vitebsk while the southern pincer erupted from the Mogilev area, and from these starting points the armored wedges drove eastward. By 26 July they had met and closed yet another cauldron, this one behind Smolensk, capturing another 348 000 Soviet soldiers and 3000 enemy tanks. Smolensk was more than 400 miles from the starting line for the German forces, and it had taken the Germans slightly more than a month to push this far into the USSR and capture almost a million Red Army soldiers. It thus appeared that the Red Army must be on the verge of collapse.

On 19 July OKW issued Directive No. 33, which ordered that after the capture of Smolensk and its pocket that the armored forces of Army Group Center would be diverted southward in support of Army Group South and northward in support of Army Group North. Hitler had never agreed that Moscow was a priority target and therefore followed his initial idea of using the army group's armor to assist the other army groups; the implication is, of course, that Hitler believed that the Red Army had been shattered in front of Army Group Center. Moscow, he said, 'is for me only a geographical concept' rather than a valid military goal, and he still believed the fall of Leningrad and Kiev would be more decisive in causing the collapse of Soviet morale than the capture of its capital. This left Army Group Center without armor and with only its infantry while it stood, virtually immobile, about 200 miles from Moscow and faced, the Germans believed, no Soviet units. The march towards Moscow, which Bock believed could be accomplished relatively easily now that Soviet forces in that direction had been destroyed (most of the one million prisoners taken since 22 June had been captured in the Bialystok–Minsk–Smolensk–Moscow axis) would now have to wait until missions elsewhere had been accomplished and the armor returned to Army Group Center.

But the Soviets, despite their massive and unprecedented losses, did not stand aside and let the Germans dictate events. Timoshenko launched an offensive in July that threatened to break the Smolensk pocket open and free the trapped forces. After considerable effort the Germans were able to defeat the attacks, but it caused considerable anxiety among German commanders because they had believed the Soviet units in the region were too exhausted and weak to attempt such an attack. The result of Timoshenko's attack was that Guderian was ordered to take his panzer group and destroy strong Soviet tank forces at Gomel, west of his present position. He was being asked, in other words, to attack westward. By 4 August Guderian had achieved his goals so thoroughly that *Stavka* panicked and ordered Yeremenko to destroy Guderian's panzers and for a week the battle raged on the Desna river in a region the Germans thought had been cleared of the Red Army. Halder, astounded that there were still Red Army units facing Army Group Center, confided to his diary on 11 August that every unit the Germans had destroyed had been replaced [**Doc. 10, p. 116**].

By the end of August Army Group Center had pushed its way hundreds of miles into the interior of the USSR. It had captured over a million prisoners, thousands of tanks and masses of equipment, and destroyed dozens of Soviet military units. It stood on the banks of the Desna and Dnepr rivers, poised to strike at Moscow. By all appearances it had accomplished the goals assigned it by 'Barbarossa,' within the plan's original time schedule (1 September was nine weeks after 22 June). But the Soviets had not yet been smashed, as Timoshenko's assault against Guderian's panzers had shown. The Germans were now at the Dnepr but had not accomplished the main goal: the destruction of the Red Army. The Soviet forces in front of Army Group Center had been battered, but there were still many strong and viable Red Army units facing the Germans, and they had thus frustrated German plans (see Map 1).

THE BATTLE FOR LENINGRAD

In the area of Army Group North the attack far exceeded even German expectations. Commanded by General Wilhelm von Leeb, it had the smallest forces but a serious task: clearing a path to and capturing Leningrad. Leeb placed his armor, unlike the other army groups, in the center of his forces so they could drive straight to Daugavpils, Pskov, and Leningrad. Speed was of the essence and Leeb ordered his formations not to 'stop for anything.' His idea was to push his armor quickly into the enemy rear to prevent defensive positions from being constructed that would slow or halt his offensive. Fourth Panzer Group was to cross the Nieman river, race for and seize the crossings over the Dvina at Daugavpils, and then continue eastward towards Pskov as rapidly as possible. Its main axis of advance took it through Lithuania, which had been integrated into the USSR only about a year earlier. It had a poor road network and serious natural obstacles, including lakes, rivers, and woodland. At many villages and towns the Germans were greeted by the population as liberators; the recent integration of the Baltic states into the Soviet Union had not eradicated nationalist feelings among the new Soviet citizens. They often greeted the Germans troops with bread and salt, the traditional gifts of welcome, as well as strewing flowers and the

Lithuanian national flag in their path (the flags had been forbidden after the integration of the Baltic states into the USSR). But the Red Army did not welcome the invaders, and like their counterparts in Army Group Center, the northern units found the Soviets to be stubborn and patient soldiers. The 126th Infantry Division, for example, was held up for three hours by a single Soviet machine gun crew, who managed to inflict serious casualties. But just as in the center, Soviet resistance rapidly crumbled in the face of surprise, superior German numbers, and skill.

In Lithuania an anti-Soviet liberation movement arose the first day of the invasion and seized several government buildings as well as a radio station in Kaunas. As the Germans approached the city (about 100 miles from the border) Soviet resistance stiffened, but their task was complicated by Lithuanian rebels who began to attack Red Army units. By 24 June advance German units were in the city, and by 26 June Kaunas was fully occupied by German troops, who had not expected such enthusiastic support. On their left flank the Germans reached the port city of Libau within one day (24 June), and for four days the Soviets waged a fierce battle for it, but it finally fell to intensive German efforts on 28 June. The German navy immediately got to work reestablishing its viability as a naval base and even salvaged a few Red Navy vessels. Lithuania proved to be an easy conquest for the Germans (see Map 1).

Anti-Semitism then emerged with a horrible vengeance as bands of Lithuanians began a pogrom against Jews in Kaunas even before the Germans had fully arrived. As the Germans occupied the city the pogrom continued under German eyes, including a nightmarish scene where Lithuanians, one of them known as the 'Death Dealer of Kaunas,' beat dozens of Jews to death with an iron rod while both Germans and Lithuanians watched. By 26 June it is estimated that 1500 Jews had been killed by both Lithuanians and Germans in Kaunas. The remainder of Kaunas' Jews (about 10 000 people) were moved to a chain of forts around the city (especially the Seventh and Ninth Forts), where by the end of July the *Einsatzgruppe* had shot them all (see Map 2).

The German advance was relatively easy but nonetheless saw some serious difficulties. On 23 June near Rossieny a Soviet tank force of 300 tanks, supported by cavalry and artillery, struck the Germans hard, with wave after wave of suicidal frontal attacks. At this battle the Germans in the north discovered the KV-1 heavy tank, already familiar to Army Group Center. The *landsers* had to improvise by moving in as close as possible (usually within a few feet) and then throwing demolition charges either onto the tracks or under the turret in order to immobilize the monsters. Wave after wave of tanks and soldiers came at the Germans, an incredible scene reminiscent of the First War which resulted in the deaths of thousands of Red Army

Landsers: The German nickname for its infantry.

soldiers. This was a stressful kind of fighting, and a major reported that panic among the Germans facing such stubborn resistance was overcome only with difficulty.

Pressing hard on the main roads the panzers reached Daugavpils, about 200 miles from the invasion point, by 26 June, as German special forces seized bridges across the Dvina river. The Soviets tried hard to destroy the vital crossings and lost 20 tanks, 20 field guns, and 17 anti-tank guns in the effort, but ultimately failed to retake the bridges.

By 1 July there was a bridgehead 18 miles across the river, and the Germans proceeded into open country towards Leningrad. The Germans then concentrated their armor at the crossing (under the command of General **Erich von Manstein**) and prepared to move towards Leningrad. The Germans broadened their bridgehead across the river by building another bridge about 50 miles further north at Yekabpils and then crossed their armor at both points en masse, advancing towards Leningrad on a broad front. By 1 July the Germans were well into Latvia and began to break through the old Soviet defensive line, called the 'Stalin Line.' Confused Soviet attacks accomplished nothing but the loss of valuable men and equipment and, by 5 July, the Germans were moving at full speed towards Pskov, their second objective.

The easy advance through Lithuania was repeated in Latvia and Estonia. The battle for Riga lasted for only about one day as the Soviets withdrew rather quickly rather than face the Germans with rebellious Latvians in their rear, as they had risen much as the Lithuanians had. Many of the ethnic Latvians serving in the Red Army deserted their units as the Red Army broke apart and fled before the Germans. These deserters then began to seize key buildings and military assets in Riga, and on 1 July these disparate forces were unified into a Latvian Defense Force which was placed under the supervision of the German army. By 7 July, as German troops crossed into Estonia, an independent and anti-communist government was formed which welcomed the Germans. By the beginning of July, less than two weeks into the war, both Lithuania and Latvia had been captured, Estonia was rapidly being overrun, and the Germans were well on their way to Leningrad.

Once the Germans had passed through the Baltic states and entered Russia, however, the advance began to slow due to terrain and increasingly well organized resistance. It was not until 20 July that the panzers had pushed beyond Pskov towards Luga and were ready for the final push towards Leningrad, 60 miles distant. But complications continued to arise, including threats on the right flank from the Soviet units caught in the enormous pockets created by Army Group Center. Army Group North had to detach units to help reduce the Bialystok and Minsk pockets, which prevented them from supporting the tanks racing for Leningrad. Army Group North was thus becoming scattered over a broad front with the tanks far

Manstein, Erich von (1887–1973): Panzer leader in Army Group North during 1941, he was moved to Army Group South to capture the Crimea. In September 1942 he was transferred to capture Leningrad, and in the fall moved to Army Group South again to save Sixth Army at Stalingrad. Placed in command of Army Group South, he conducted the withdrawals to the Dnepr until relieved of command in April 1944.

ahead and the infantry far behind and OKH became concerned, due to the experiences of Army Group Center, about the gap between the mobile forces and the foot soldiers. To correct this the panzers, which had driven hundreds of miles by this point, slowed their advance so that the infantry could catch up.

By the end of July it was decided that the operation to take Leningrad would be accomplished with the tanks and infantry working together rather than through armored spearheads. The assault, which began on 8 August, saw heavy fighting which prevented a breakthrough until 12 August, but exploitation of this apparent German victory was delayed when a portion of the armor was sent southward to Staraya Russa to rescue German units in serious trouble of being encircled. Army Group North thus had to slow the pace of its operations, just like Army Group Center, in order to protect its flanks from Soviet incursions. Hitler, hoping to free the mobile forces for an advance into Leningrad, detached part of a panzer group from Army Group Center to assist Army Group North in closing the gaps in its front lines and cleaning up the threats to its right flank. These attacks were successful, but it was not until 31 August that the flanks were cleared and the offensive against Leningrad could begin in earnest. While these loose ends were being tied the defenders of Leningrad had been given about three weeks to prepare for the inevitable German assault. The offensive against Leningrad finally began on 8 September and, despite desperate resistance, German units had reached the Volkhov river by 17 September, cutting Leningrad off from land communications with the rest of the USSR.

But the Germans did not have the offensive power to storm and capture what was an important city strategically, politically, and symbolically. All of Army Group North's armor (not just the units borrowed from Army Group Center) were withdrawn at this time for the assault on Moscow, and Manstein, whose units were sent to Moscow, said after the war that the constant movement of armor between army groups just when it seemed that a breakthrough could be achieved in one place or another made no sense to him, and it was unclear what purpose German strategy served. With the loss of its mobile units progress against the city began to taper off and the fighting settled into a siege rather than a direct assault upon the city. By the end of September Hitler preferred to starve the city rather than risk men and equipment in an assault and Army Group North settled down to the longest siege of the war, the very opposite of mobile tank warfare. A strike by Fourth Panzer around 25 July might have put the panzers in a position to take the city, as its defenses were still being developed at that time, but the multifarious tasks of Army Group North in aid of its neighbor as well as it own tasks on a broadening front made it difficult to focus on Leningrad, its main effort. The Finns, who were also fighting in the northern sector, were content with recovering the territory lost during their war with the USSR in 1939–40 and never really considered Leningrad a military goal. Army Group North had made spectacular progress but in the end failed to accomplish its one goal for 'Operation Barbarossa:' it never captured Leningrad.

THE BATTLE FOR KIEV

Donbas: The Don and Donets river basin in the Ukraine. A rich industrial and agricultural area highly desired by both sides during the war.

Rokossovsky, Konstantin (1896–1968): Soviet army commander who participated in the defense of Moscow, the encirclement at Stalingrad, Kursk, 'Operation Bagration,' and the capture of Berlin.

Reichenau, Walther von (1884–1942): German Field Marshal who was a devoted adherent to the ideals of Nazism, he commanded Sixth Army (Army Group South) until November, 1941 when he succeeded Rundstedt as commander of Army Group South. He issued notoriously anti-Semitic orders to the troops of his army which were sent by Hitler to the other army commanders. Died of a heart attack.

Kleist, Ewald von (1881 –1954): Commander of the First Panzer Group of Army Group South in June 1941. Participated in some of the largest operations on the Eastern Front, including leading the forces in the Caucasus during 'Operation Blue.' Relieved of command after his perceived failure to hold the Crimea in 1944.

Army Group South faced a different war than its counterparts to the north. Not only did the Soviets expect the main thrust to occur south of the Pripet marshes and had therefore positioned the majority of its finest units there, but crossing the Bug river also posed serious obstacles. The army group had two main missions: Sixth Army was to punch a hole for First Panzer Group to exploit by heading for the Dnepr south of Kiev, while Seventeenth Army was to drive easterly towards a linkup with First Panzer. The goal was to encircle and destroy all units west of Kiev and the Dnepr before they could withdraw across the river. The linchpin of the whole region was Kiev, capital of the Ukraine and a gateway to Kharkov and the **Donbas**, the basin of the Don and Donets rivers where a vast industrial and agricultural network existed.

In order to prevent the Germans from piercing their front and encircling their forces, the Soviet commanders threw their tank formations into the border battles. But these units were unprepared for the fast moving mobile warfare being waged by the Germans. Commanders had insufficient information about the ebb and flow of the battle and often sent conflicting and contradictory orders to subordinate units; the VIII Mechanized Corps received orders which kept it flitting in one direction after another for three days without ever putting it in a location from which it could engage the Germans. By the time it finally met German forces it had lost half of its vehicles to mechanical breakdowns and had lost much of its fighting capabilities. By 27 June the Soviets, under **Konstantin Rokossovsky**, finally managed to put a capable force together which, although defeated and repulsed, managed to slow the Germans down for about a week.

The German Sixth Army, commanded by Field Marshal **Walther von Reichenau**, met such fierce resistance during its advance to the north of Lvov that it ordered all prisoners to be shot as partisans. Alongside this infantry army drove the tanks of **Ewald von Kleist**'s panzer group, which made better progress and soon bypassed Lvov heading for Rovno, threatening to encircle all Soviet forces further west. The Soviets planned to stop these pincers by launching an armored counterattack, but the units were scattered across the front and had difficulty assembling for the attack. Natural obstacles complicated their tasks to the point that some units, including an entire division, became lost in swamps. When the attack was finally launched on 23 June it lasted for four days and saw intensive fighting between the *Luftwaffe*, German and Soviet tanks, and the infantry on both sides. But poor communications between Soviet infantry units and tanks precluded an effective effort, and German attempts to bypass resistance and capture Red Army supply bases caused insuperable difficulties for the Soviets.

The panzers were therefore able to capture Lvov on 30 June and unhinge the entire Soviet front. Hungary, now convinced that Germany would win the war, declared war on the USSR on 27 June, followed the next day by Albania. Both nations provided a small number of forces for the Eastern Front under the command of Army Group South, and while their contribution was negligible it permitted Germany to trumpet the war as a multinational anticommunist effort.

On 2 July the second half of Army Group South's operations commenced with an attack into Moldova. The plan was to swing these forces northward to trap the Soviet defenders in a cauldron and then eliminate them. The powerful Southern *Front* managed to erect a formidable defensive barrier between the Dnestr and Pruth rivers, and the German effort made little progress. As Sixth Army advanced towards Berdichev and Zhitomir it ran into heavy resistance but managed, with the assistance of the panzers, to force the shattered remnants to flee to the vast Pripet marshes to the north. By 11 July the lead panzer units were only ten miles from Kiev but were halted by their commander to await the arrival of the infantry. Rundstedt decided that Kiev should be taken by envelopment, but this was too ambitious as there was a 150-mile gap between his army group and Army Group Center, and in this area Soviet forces roamed virtually unchallenged. The offensive towards Kiev was therefore halted so that Sixth Army could deal with this threat on its flank. OKW then decided to eliminate all threats to the southern flank of Army Group Center by sending its panzer forces southward towards Chernigov while Army Group South's panzers were moved from Kremenchug northward in order to close the yawning gap between the army groups. This maneuver had the added benefit of permitting an envelopment of Kiev by both army groups. The commander of Southwest *Front* interpreted this as a drive into his rear and asked for permission to withdraw in order to forestall an encirclement. *Stavka*, however, denied this request and instead created a new *front*, the Bryansk *Front*, with Yeremenko in command. But Kleist and Guderian, commanding the pincers driving from Chernigov and Kremenchug, sliced through Yeremenko's forces and linked up at Lokhvitsa, about 100 miles east of Kiev. While Sixth Army pressed in from the west an enormous pocket of over 650 000 Soviet soldiers was created east of Kiev. By 24 September most of the men inside were either killed, including the commander of Southwest *Front*, or captured. This was the largest encirclement battle in the history of warfare.

In the Kiev pocket 50 Soviet divisions disappeared and the entire front was smashed open. It was the greatest victory thus far and, paradoxically, a strategic blunder on the part of the Germans. For eight weeks the powerful units of Army Group Center sat defensively idle just east of Smolensk while its armor drove to close the Kiev pocket. While it remained immobile, strong Soviet attacks continually whittled away its strength and by the time the tanks and infantry were reunited valuable time had been lost and irreplaceable men and equipment lost or damaged; and still the Red Army had not been destroyed.

The loss of Kiev made Soviet resistance west of the Dnepr impossible. Odessa, which had held out thus far, was finally taken on 16 October as Eleventh Army drove towards the neck of the Crimea; this created yet another pocket of Soviet prisoners just northeast of Odessa and unhinged the entire Soviet defensive system in the south.

THE FIRST MAJOR GERMAN DEFEAT: ROSTOV

As Army Group South pushed eastward after its victory at Kiev it was exhilarated but weakened. Its next major goal, Rostov, was a great distance from its current position. First Panzer had only around 300 tanks by this time, and the infantry had suffered enormous casualties. From the viewpoint of Southern and Southwestern *Fronts* the outlook was ominous, however, as the Germans were poised to seize the most industrially and agriculturally productive regions of the USSR. The German goal was to break First Panzer out towards the Sea of Azov, encircling three Soviet armies (the entire Southern *Front*) and placing the Germans in an excellent position to continue to the Volga. On 30 September the race began as First Panzer aimed for the main Soviet rail line from Kharkov to Zaporozhye, which was reached and cut by 1 October. By 6 October the Germans had closed another pocket between Orekhov and Osipenko, trapping over 100 000 Soviets and clearing the field all the way to Rostov. *Stavka*, in the meantime, planned to stop the Germans by pulling back to a more defensible line closer to Rostov and by deploying a new army (Thirty-seventh Army) whose main job was to counterattack into the flanks of the Germans. Further north the Germans prepared to take Kharkov; Rundstedt wanted to envelop the city with infantry pincers north and south of the city since his panzers were further south. *Stavka* realized the dangers, however, and abandoned the city on 24 October in order to save the armies fighting in the region. The Germans captured the city, but caught almost no prisoners and destroyed no major units in the process. The Soviets were beginning to learn how to avoid annihilating combat, thanks in part to the battle for Kiev.

On 1 November First Panzer opened its main offensive towards Rostov. A series of defensive belts and the well-fortified positions slowed the armor as it tried to move eastward; in addition the weather degenerated and mud and ice hampered the activities of both sides. First Panzer was able to gain only very short distances as late as 12 November (by then they were moving only five miles a day), and its supply columns were having trouble keeping sufficient supplies on hand (even such necessities as boots could not be replaced in sufficient quantities). The full-scale assault on Rostov itself began on 17 November, despite intense snow storms and bitter cold. Within two days the Germans were in the northern suburbs, but on 19 November Timoshenko ordered Thirty-seventh Army into action.

As Rostov was cleared of Soviet units and finally captured on 21 November, Thirty-seventh Army bore down on a gap between the German units, threatening to divide and encircle them; for the first time in the war Soviet units were about to envelop major German formations. But the Soviet army lacked the mobility to drive quickly to Taganrog and complete the encirclement, and by 27 November the Germans realized the danger they faced. First Panzer erected a strong defensive line to allow the other German units to escape westward and then fled Rostov itself on 29 November. Rundstedt, correctly foreseeing Soviet plans, tried to prevent the encirclement of his army group by withdrawing to the Mius river and abandoning Taganrog. He had failed to seek approval of his retreat, however, and when Hitler learned of it he immediately ordered that Taganrog not be abandoned. Rundstedt, who considered this an extremely dangerous position, refused to cancel his orders and was sacked by Hitler (officially he went on sick leave); his replacement was Reichenau, the commander of Sixth Army. Reichenau realized the survival of the army group depended upon the withdrawal and managed to convince Hitler to permit him to complete the withdrawal before the Germans were surrounded and destroyed. The drive to Rostov resulted in the irreplaceable loss of men, equipment, time, prestige (this was their first major defeat), and Rundstedt, who never served on the Eastern Front again.

The victory at Rostov was the first major Soviet victory of the war. The Caucasus and much of the Donbas had been saved from German occupation, but most importantly it was demonstrated that the Germans could be defeated. The image of the *Wehrmacht* as an unbeatable foe had been seriously tarnished; not only did Soviet soldiers acquire a sense of confidence but the victory at Rostov also, to some degree, made it less clear to Turkey that Germany was winning the war and caused the Germans a loss of prestige both domestically and abroad. It also definitively demonstrated to the Germans that the Red Army had not been destroyed west of the Dnepr, and that despite the incredible losses of the preceding weeks the Red Army remained a dangerous foe.

Despite these setbacks the first few weeks of 'Barbarossa' were extremely successful by any measure. The victories near the borders had smashed dozens of Soviet formations and created the impression among German commanders that the Soviets had few resources remaining at their disposal. It also appeared that despite isolated instances of robust resistance that most of the German units advanced against very little organized opposition. Dozens of cities and entire regions were enveloped and surrounded by the Germans as they chewed Soviet military formations to pieces. But neither Leningrad nor Moscow had been taken; Kiev had been taken but at great cost; and still the Red Army survived. German planners, however, stuck to 'Barbarossa' and decided to refocus their attention on Moscow, hoping to complete the annihilation of the Red Army.

MASS MURDER IN THE USSR

In order to more fully understand the war on the Eastern Front it is crucial to keep in mind that the *Einsatzgruppen* quickly followed upon the heels of the army as it advanced into the Soviet Union. As cities and regions were conquered and the army continued to move eastward, these SS units arrived to carry out their 'special tasks' (see Plate 1) Each *gruppe* had its own area of operation: *Einsatzgruppe* A was assigned to the Baltic countries; *Einsatzgruppe* B was sent further south into Belorussia; *Einsatzgruppe* C was assigned to one portion of the Ukraine while *Einsatzgruppe* D was assigned the rest of the Ukraine. The largest unit was *Einsatzgruppe* A, with about 900 men, while *Einsatzgruppe* D was the smallest at around 500 men. Each *gruppe* was further divided into *kommandos*, smaller detachments able to carry out their tasks while dispersed from the main group.

In 1939 the region of Zhitomir had about 260 000 Jews and was one of the largest centers of Jewish culture in the USSR. This was widely known even by the Germans, who planned to destroy the whole area as a 'Jewish-Bolshevik' center. On 25 July 1941, about two weeks after Zhitomir was captured, all Jews in a nearby village aged 16–60 were murdered. About a month later *Einsatzgruppe* C began systematically rounding up all Jews in the region and shooting them. In Berdichev, for example, 23 000 people were killed between 26 August and 16 September. On 19 September the *gruppe* killed over 5000 Jews in Vinnitsa and another 15 000 in Berdichev. One of the most notorious killings occurred on 7 August, when Sixth Army personnel in Zhitomir rounded up 400 male Jews to watch a public hanging. Ukrainians in the crowd were then encouraged to assault the 400 men, who were finally loaded into trucks, taken to a prepared ditch outside of town, and shot by soldiers, the *SS*, and Ukrainian volunteers (Lower, 2005).

On 7 July Army Group Center ordered Jews within its sector to be registered and to wear the yellow star. Further orders required them to move into specific ghettos in certain cities. In Minsk this meant the relocation of thousands of people (Heer, 2000 (1)). On 5 October 1941 the 286th Security Division operating behind Army Group Center entered the village of Krupka and shot over 1000 Jews, including women and children. As the murders were committed, other Jews were moved into the area in order to be available for murder; for example, in October the *Wehrmacht* shot about 8000 Jews in the Minsk area to make room for German Jews from Hamburg, who arrived on 8 November. These people were in turn shot during June 1942 (Heer, 2000 (1)). On 20 October 7000 Jews from Borisov were shot, and in November another 5000 were shot at Bobruisk.

Often these were shot on the pretext of being 'partisans,' even though there was no organized or effective partisan movement in 1941. Army Group Center reported that as of December 1941 it had shot 19 000 'partisans and criminals,' with another 20 000 shot during the first half of 1942 (Heer, 2000 (1): 72). 'Operation Bamberg,' an anti-partisan operation by Army Group Center during March and April 1942, resulted in 3500 'partisans and their helpers' being shot at a loss of six Germans killed. Clearly these people were, for the most part, unarmed and were thus simply murdered and not killed in combat. Another example of this mentality occurred in December 1941, when Sixth Army began destroying all of the villages within a few miles of its front lines, forcing the inhabitants out into the open during the winter. This of course resulted in a large number of deaths from exposure, but it also created a vast number of 'tramps' who were then shot as 'partisans' by security units further west (Boll and Safrian, 2000). The litany of atrocities behind the operational area of Army Group Center reads like a virtual list of the towns captured: on 2–3 October over 7000 Jews were murdered in Mogilev; during October another 3000 were shot in Vitebsk and in Borisov 7000 people were murdered. In the area of Army Group North 26 000 Jews were killed in Riga between 30 November and 8 December; and in Vilnius 12 388 during October and November (Megargee, 2006: 122–3).

In fact Sixth Army serves as a useful case study of the German advance into the USSR and the treatment of Soviet citizens, both Jewish and Christian. As it crossed the Ukraine on the way to its destiny at Stalingrad, it committed a vast number of atrocities, both large and small. The 'Guidelines for Troop Behavior' issued by the army was sent by the commanders of Sixth Army down to the division level, and the shooting of political commissars was 'routine' among its units (Boll and Safrian, 2000). Very early on the divisional commanders included 'irregulars' among those shot, most of whom were in fact Jews. On 19 July 1941 Sixth Army ordered that whenever the actual culprits of partisan attacks could not be located and punished, that local Jews would be shot in their place (Boll and Safrian, 2000). Elements of *Einsatzgruppen* C accompanied Sixth Army units, and in October 1941 these reported that they had shot 55 432 people, mostly Jews. At Lutsk an orgy of violence was unleashed which resulted in the murder of 1160 people by 2 July. In mid-August the Sixth Army commander in the village of Belaya Tsukov ordered the registration of all Jews, and then once that had been completed turned them all over to the *Einsatzgruppe* to be murdered. A group of 90 children had been locked into a barn and not shot, and these had become such a problem for the army (all of the adults had been murdered) that on 21 August Reichenau ordered their murder (Boll and Safrian, 2000).

The most notorious of Sixth Army's role in mass murder occurred in the Kiev region in September 1941. On 21 September the Sixth Army commander of Kiev ordered all Jews to be relocated to another town; they were thus ordered to appear at a public square and bring their valuables with them for resettlement on 29 September. After they had assembled they were then turned over to the *Einsatzgruppe*, *Waffen-SS* units, and a police battalion, who took them into a ravine outside of the city at Babi Yar and murdered all 33 000 of them over the next two days, 29–30 September (see Plate 2). Sixth Army also left a bloody footprint at Kharkov: after an explosion in the city killed a few German soldiers in November 1941, all Jews in the region were relocated to an old factory and during December 1941 and January 1942 were shot or killed by carbon monoxide poisoning (Boll and Safrian, 2000).

At the end of 1941 the *Einsatzgruppen* submitted their action reports and revealed that almost 500 000 people had been murdered in the areas conquered by the *Wehrmacht*, including 250 000 by *Einsatzgruppe* A; 45 000 by *Einsatzgruppe* B; 95 000 by *Einsatzgruppe* C; and 92 000 by *Einsatzgruppe* D. These figures do not include those killed by the army or police battalions in the rear areas, and the true figure for those murdered during the second half of 1941 is much higher, perhaps even double the reported total. It is therefore crucial, as part of a more thorough comprehension of the Eastern Front, to understand that these murders continued throughout the remainder of the war (see Plate 3).

THE BATTLE FOR MOSCOW

By the early fall Hitler decided that Moscow was an important goal after all and planning commenced for an operation to seize the capital; this would be the moment, Hitler thought, when the Red Army would finally be destroyed.

Army Group Center had in the meantime remained immobile for nearly two months, and *Stavka* had taken frantic measures to erect formidable defensive works around the city. The importance of the battle for Moscow upon German and Soviet perceptions of the war cannot be overrated; for example German General Hasso von Manteuffel believed that after the battle for Moscow whatever Hitler 'undertook from this time on could only delay his ultimate downfall' (Jukes, 1970). Manstein expressed the common German viewpoint of the battle when he explained that the defeat was caused by 'Hitler overextending his armies, mud, and the winter' (Liddell Hart, 1956: 141). But Manstein and other generals also admitted that the real cause of defeat was the toughness of Soviet soldiers and that the 'German political and military leaders had greatly underrated Soviet strength and fighting determination' (Liddell Hart, 1956: 139). These may be the opinions of the Germans who fought the battle, but they omitted one of the most important factors: inadequate planning and preparation on the part of the German command.

The plan for the assault on Moscow, code named '**Operation Typhoon,**' envisioned Fourth Army and Fourth Panzer advancing along the Roslavl–Moscow road, while Ninth Army and Third Panzer moved eastward via the Smolensk–Moscow road. The two groups would swing together in front of Moscow at Vyazma, creating a pocket which trapped and destroyed most of the Soviet units in front of Moscow. Second Army and Second Panzer were to repeat this operation further south, trapping another large group of Soviet armies at Bryansk. These pincers would then lunge forward north and south of Moscow, reach beyond the capital, and then clamp shut again somewhere east of the city, trapping the last formations of the Red Army in the Soviet Union.

'Operation Typhoon:' The German codeword for the assault against Moscow in the late fall of 1941.

The offensive was divided into two phases, the southern pincer began on 30 September while the northern armies began on 2 October. The envelopment at Vyazma, one of the largest in military history, was achieved relatively quickly while Guderian's Second Panzer and Second Army closed their pincers around Bryansk by 6 October. Hundreds of thousands of Soviet prisoners were taken in these huge envelopments, but the pockets took a great deal of time to clear of their prisoners. It was only on 20 October that they were eliminated, netting a total prisoner count of around 650 000 and destroying eight Soviet armies. By mid-October it thus looked very promising for the Germans.

Leaving the infantry behind to clear the pockets, Second Panzer then struck for the major armaments center at Tula on 7 October while Fourth Panzer drove for Mozhaisk, 60 miles from Moscow. On 12 October Hitler, confident of victory, ordered that the surrender of Moscow would not be accepted and that 'it would be utterly irresponsible to risk the lives of German soldiers to save Russian towns from fires or to feed their population at Germany's expense.' Moscow was therefore not to be captured, but encircled and then starved into submission rather than occupied by force (there were even plans to bomb it into oblivion and then flood the area so as to completely wipe it off the face of the earth; of course this meant that all of its inhabitants would be killed). As October progressed the mood in the capital became desperate as the Muscovites waited for word that the city was surrounded, while the government and diplomatic corps were evacuated on 16 October. Even Stalin considered evacuation but in the end, after reassurances from Zhukov that Moscow would not fall, decided it was safe to stay (Bellamy, 2007).

Rasputitsa: Literally, the 'time without roads.' A Russian term to describe the rainy periods during the fall and spring when the roads became merely mud.

But heavy rains signaled the arrival of the *rasputitsa*, the 'time without roads.' Since most Soviet roads were unpaved, the heavy fall and spring rains turned them into impassable mud holes. Extremely thick and clinging mud made even the simplest of movement nearly impossible and exhausted men, animals, machines, and fuel (see Plate 4). Vehicles with wheels could move only if dragged by tracked vehicles such as tanks, and animals began dying by the thousands from overwork. The incredible effort required just to move slowed the entire front to a crawl. By the end of October the *Wehrmacht* was in serious trouble: many of its divisions were at only half strength, while the tanks were gradually worn out and, since there were few repair facilities, abandoned. By early November the 17 panzer divisions involved in the offensive had the same number of tanks that six would have had in June; one of Guderian's corps had only 50 of its original 600 tanks. The highly mobile Germans, who relied upon their vehicles to execute vast encircling maneuvers, were losing their ability to move around the battlefield.

And then came the cold: on 6 November snow began to fall in the Moscow area. The mud, thankfully, began to freeze and it was possible to extricate the equipment and move again, but the Germans had planned for a war lasting 8–10 weeks and had not, therefore, prepared for a winter war. In addition to a serious lack of winter-grade lubricants for vehicles and weapons, German supply units had only enough winter uniforms for what was supposed to have been, by now, an occupation force much smaller than the invading army. Most German soldiers had to continue wearing, in winter conditions, the same summer-weight uniforms they had worn when they invaded in June. In addition the supply lines, never established on firm foundations, were at the breaking point which Paulus had predicted before the war. The railways, already overtaxed at the beginning of the war, were now incapable of keeping the men supplied with ammunition and fuel, without which they would perish, let alone food, uniforms, or the other necessities of life. The trucks upon which Hitler and the top commanders placed their hopes had suffered tremendous losses since June which had not been made up, and the *rasputitsa* had placed such an enormous mechanical and physical stress on the vehicles and animals that it was extremely difficult to move anything at all by early November despite the end of the rainy season.

The Germans were experiencing so much trouble achieving their goals that they began venting their frustrations in a crescendo of violence; in the south Reichenau ordered Sixth Army to shed its inhibitions and shoot any civilians or combatants who threatened them, especially Jews [**Doc. 11, p. 116**]. By 30 October Guderian reached the outskirts of Tula, but he could not attack it because of a lack of supplies and mobility. Soviet attacks along the left flank of Army Group South, which was supposed to protect the right flank of Army Group Center as it advanced towards Moscow, opened an 80 mile gap between Army Group South and Army Group Center. Guderian's units, which occupied that right flank of Army Group Center, had therefore both to take Tula and close the gap, but the shortage of men and equipment meant it was unable to move. Despite these serious problems, Bock ordered the envelopment of Moscow by sending Second Panzer to positions on the Moskva river, parts of Fourth Army and Third and Fourth Panzer to the Volga canal, and Ninth Army to Kalinin. Once these positions had been reached, they were to close the pincers around Moscow by pushing eastward. But these movements required a mobility which the German army no longer possessed. The Germans expended enormous effort and resources trying to move into the positions necessary to surround Moscow, but simply could not avoid the physical realities or break growing Soviet resistance. On 29 October Hitler, realizing how immobile his army had become, tried to assuage his fears by deriding mobility as 'unusable,' but this was merely self-delusional [**Doc. 12, p. 117**].

By the beginning of November it was clear that 'Typhoon' was increasingly a distant dream. On 11 November Halder, recognizing the truth, said that 'the time for spectacular operational feats is past' (Halder, 1988: 556). The German conceptual approach thus far in the war, that vast enveloping movements performed quickly won wars, was therefore dropped in favor of tactical maneuvers to achieve limited goals. Army Group Center now believed the effort to capture Moscow had so overstretched its forces that a break of several weeks was necessary in order to resupply, regroup, and rest the men. The prewar underestimation of the Soviets combined with unrealistic expectations of German capabilities had thus merged with the lack of motorized transport to confront the German commanders with a problem: what to do next.

OKH tried to figure out its next step by holding a meeting of all the top eastern commanders at Orsha on 13 November. Halder, like Hitler, hoped the cold weather would permit a few more weeks for operations and suggested that the situation presented two choices: stop and conserve the army's strength for a future offensive (the desire of Army Group Center), or make an all-out last effort. Hitler and Halder preferred the latter and tried to persuade the commanders to adopt it. During the conference Halder's aides revealed that the army would not be able to replace its losses thus far in either men or vehicles, and that the infantry divisions would have to be completely stripped of all motor vehicles and nearly half of all supply columns would have to be horse-drawn in order to maintain acceptable levels of motorization in the armored forces. Halder was trying to suggest that the army could not, no matter which path it chose, hope to re-motorize in the future. He painted an equally grim picture for ammunition and heavy equipment and tried to make it clear that the future, and therefore the postponement of 'Typhoon,' held no happy prospects. The army commanders then presented their arguments to Halder; Guderian, for example, doubted whether any of his units except his tanks could even move, let alone lead an envelopment of Moscow. The commanders tried to persuade Halder that the ambitious goals of 'Typhoon' were unrealizable during 1941 because of the physical realities at the front. But Hitler and Halder got their way and operations to envelop Moscow not only went ahead but continued for another three weeks. But at Orsha it was clear that 'Operation Barbarossa' had failed and that the armies would have to continue the war into 1942 (Ziemke, 1975).

By 27 November the lead panzers were only about 20 miles from central Moscow, but by that time had run into so many difficulties that they requested assistance from Fourth Army, which was having its own problems and could offer no help. By late November the attack had ground to a halt everywhere as supplies ran short, fuel ran out, and the men were simply exhausted by the sheer effort and cold. On 1 December a frontal assault was launched down the Moscow–Minsk highway (one of the few major paved roads in the USSR), but strong Soviet attacks forced it to a halt, and by 8 December Hitler, recognizing that 'Typhoon' had failed, issued Directive No. 39 [**Doc. 13, p. 118**], which blamed a 'surprisingly early' winter and the severe cold on the difficulties facing the Germans. The entire Eastern Front ground to a halt and went over to the defensive. Both 'Operation Barbarossa' and 'Operation Typhoon' had failed.

But the war was far from over, and in fact Zhukov and *Stavka* had planned a surprise for the Germans. Rather than throwing all available reserves into the maw of Moscow, the Soviet command built strong reserves which it deployed north and south of the city beyond the front so that the Germans would not discover their existence. Zhukov pulled a total of 18 divisions and 1700 tanks from the far east in order to carry out an ambitious offensive designed to destroy Army Group Center's pincers aimed at enveloping Moscow. The plan was to sever the armored pincers and then wheel around the German formations from both the north and the south to a meeting point roughly at Smolensk, thus encircling the entire Army Group in a cauldron.

It was designed, in other words, to destroy the entire German center. On 5 December the first of the attacks began and in subsequent days a series of operations combined into a major offensive across the entire Moscow region. Three *fronts* (Kalinin, Western, and Southwestern) participated in this epic struggle through the ice and snow, and by 13 December had pushed the Germans in the north as much as 100 miles westward and ended the threat to Moscow posed by the northern pincer.

As the Germans fell back from Moscow, Hitler realized it would be virtually impossible to recapture these areas once the Soviet offensive had been stopped. The grim picture painted at Orsha had been accurate: to delay the capture of Moscow was not a viable option and the recapture of the areas lost to the Red Army would be too costly. Hitler therefore ordered that all positions, no matter how exposed to the weather or the enemy, were to be held at all costs. No withdrawals were to be permitted until either ammunition had been exhausted or all the men killed. The stress caused by the apparent failure of German plans for 1941 caused Hitler to search for scapegoats, and during December 1941 Bock, Guderian, Leeb, and **Walther von Brauchitsch** lost their commands. The most important of these retirements was that of Brauchitsch, the head of all armed forces; his replacement on 19 December by Hitler himself created the unique situation of combining the head of state and the minister for war into the person of one man.

Brauchitsch, Walther von (1881–1948): Commander in chief of the German army from 1938 until his retirement in December 1941, when Hitler took over his position.

As Zhukov pushed the Germans relentlessly back from Moscow, Stalin decided the time was ripe to coordinate an offensive along the entire front. The battle plan for Moscow envisioned a three-phase attack with the ultimate goal of driving the Germans back to Smolensk. But this was not enough: the Germans would have to be destroyed everywhere. Stalin outlined a plan whereby Leningrad and Northwestern *Fronts* would destroy Army Group North through an envelopment of its rear, while Kalinin and Western *Fronts* would, in conjunction with Volkhov *Front*, destroy Army Group Center. Southern and Southwestern *Fronts* were to destroy Army Group South. The idea was to prevent the Germans from recuperating from the debacle at Moscow and create an unsustainable level of attrition among German units (see Plate 5).

The general offensives began on 7 January 1942 all along the Eastern Front. In addition to its own resources, the USSR relied upon Lend-Lease aid from the British, which had begun to arrive at the front lines in the early fall of 1941. While it was never decisive, the materiel given by the British contributed significant resources to the defense of Moscow during the late fall and early winter, especially in terms of medium tanks, as about one-third of those available at Moscow had been provided by the British (Hill, 2007). While not pivotal, these assets made important contributions to the defense of Moscow and the offensives in January. In the north Leningrad and Volkhov

Fronts pushed German units back to the Volkhov river but were unable to lift the siege of the city. In the center the Germans were pushed back from Moscow towards Smolensk, Vitebsk, and Vyazma, but the fighting was heavy enough that Soviet units became bogged down and slowed their advance. In the southern sector of the center region the Germans were pushed out of their advanced positions to just east of Orel and Kursk, erasing the southern pincers and removing the threat to Moscow for the remainder of the war. In the south little progress was made except south of Kharkov, where a small bridgehead permitted the Soviets to create a salient into German positions.

By 31 March the Red Army had blunted the German advance into the USSR, humiliated Hitler and the German commanders, and recovered large regions from the German occupiers. The victories came at a very high human cost: the official Soviet estimate was 926 244 irrevocably lost and another 1 800 000 wounded and sick men. But 'Operation Barbarossa' had failed, not least because of flawed planning. Not only were German hopes of destroying the Red Army west of the major rivers dashed but the Soviets had been able to bring up an enormous number of replacements for the forces swallowed in the inferno of combat. By the time the Germans reached their original goal of the Dnepr there were still very powerful fighting units blocking their way eastward. This critical failure not only ruined hopes of a successful conclusion to operations in 1941 but posed serious questions about the future. Hitler largely failed to realize what had really happened and tended to blame the weather [**Doc. 14, p. 118**]. That this was a gross simplification is probably best demonstrated by the battle for Moscow: the exhausted Germans had not only failed to destroy the Red Army and encircle Moscow, but were themselves nearly destroyed. The war was becoming a war of attrition, a type of war the Germans knew they could not fight. By the end of 1941 the Germans had suffered 917 985 casualties (nearly one-third of the invasion force in June) and were losing tanks at the rate of about 400 a month (or the entire tank force in June in less than nine months). This amounted to 155 000 men a month, or over 3000 men every single day after June 22 (Hayward, 1998). This was a rate of loss which could not be sustained by the Germans.

3

The War turns against the Germans, 1942–43

'OPERATION BLUE'

After weathering the Soviet offensives of the spring of 1942 the German high command prepared for the resumption of its campaign in the east. The order of 8 December had put the Eastern Front on the defensive in order to prepare for the 'resumption of large-scale offensive operations in 1942,' but the lack of supplies and military power made it impossible for the Germans to launch an offensive along the entire front. Instead, the Germans would have to pick a critically strategic region and devote their efforts to accomplishing its capture. The Soviets believed the main effort would come in the Moscow region, that the Germans would again try to capture the capital and sever the communications routes between the northern and southern regions. This operation would have made sense and was certainly a valid military and political goal, but Hitler had other plans in mind.

For Hitler the economic considerations of the war, always a vital factor in his calculations, now took on a newly enhanced role. He knew that Germany lacked the economic resources to fight a prolonged war against the USSR and had, relatively soon, to rectify this crippling handicap. One of the most serious shortages was the lack of petroleum products, especially fuel oil. Hitler knew that the Soviet Union relied for a great deal of its oil on the Caucasus region south of Stalingrad and that if the Germans captured this area two blows could be inflicted: the Germans would gain valuable oil resources and the Soviets would lose them. This might be enough to tip the balance in Germany's favor and lead to victory. Hitler therefore chose the area of Army Group South as the main effort in 1942.

In many ways the choice Hitler made reflected the narrowing options available to the Germans after the failure of 'Barbarossa.' The goal for 1941 had included the destruction of Soviet forces; in 1942 the primary goal was the capture of economic assets rather than the purely military goal of annihilating enemy forces (which had proven extremely elusive). The Germans, of course, hoped to repeat the spectacular successes of the previous year by launching enveloping operations which would lead to the capture of entire enemy armies, but the focus was on the capture of the Caucasus oil fields rather than destroying enemy units.

'Operation Blue:' The German codeword for the offensive into the Caucasus and Stalingrad during the summer of 1942.

'Operation Blue' was thus the result of the failure of 'Operation Barbarossa,' but it also reflected the changing nature of the war after the entry of the United States in December 1941. The war was no longer a European war but a world war with the resources of three of the great powers (Britain, the United States, and the USSR) arrayed against the Germans. If Germany hoped to win this war it must have access to sufficient natural resources, especially oil, or in the long run it faced almost certain defeat. The goal of 'Operation Blue,' besides the destruction of the USSR, was to acquire the economic resources which would permit Germany to continue the war against the Soviet Union but, just as importantly, create the conditions whereby it could successfully resist Anglo-American intervention through a second front in western Europe. If Germany could capture the resources of the Caucasus it could defend itself in the long run and make British (and American) victory less likely. Thus the strike into the Caucasus made the most strategic sense as it had the chance of knocking both the USSR and Britain out of the war (Wegner, 1997). The resources seized during 'Blue' were thus perceived as creating the strategic conditions by which Germany could hope to endure a prolonged war against Britain, the United States, and the USSR.

This was an operation of extreme risks, as it not only exposed Army Group South to potential disaster but left the belly of Army Group Center exposed to Soviet thrusts in case of disaster in the south. But the Germans had no real alternative: a defensive stance would have brought a slow drain on German resources while a renewed attack on Moscow or Leningrad not only did not guarantee victory but offered no relief from the daunting economic problems facing the Germans. Complicating the decision was the mistaken belief, held by everyone from Hitler to the intelligence agencies, that the Red Army was at the end of its strength, just like the *Wehrmacht*, and needed only a few more powerful blows before it would collapse. But the assessment of available Soviet forces by German intelligence agencies was one of the most serious blunders of the war and was proven, once fighting began, to be off by a factor of several magnitudes (Citino, 2007).

On 5 April 1942 Hitler issued Directive No. 41 [**Doc. 15, p. 119**], which focused on economic realities rather than ideological fantasies. It laid down the goal of the offensive as 'far as possible to deprive [the Soviets] of the most important sources of strength of their war economy.' Army Group Center was to remain on the defensive while Army Group North continued its attempts to capture Leningrad, while in the south Army Group South would break into the Caucasus to seize the oil fields. For once German abilities were realistically assessed and the order states that since the capture of Leningrad and the Caucasus could not be realized simultaneously, the main effort would at first be from Army Group South, as its success offered the greatest potential reward. As favorable events developed the other army groups could try to reach their objectives, especially the capture of Leningrad.

The seizure of the Caucasus, however, required that Soviet units in the region had to be neutralized. The German high command therefore envisioned destroying the Red Army rather than permitting it to withdraw and survive. Army Group South was to accomplish this between the Donets and Don rivers and then proceed across the Donbas for the western bank of the Don, where it was to erect a powerful defensive barrier along its western banks to prevent any surviving Soviet units from interfering with operations further south. This phase of the operation was thus designed to protect the long left flank which extended to the area of Stalingrad. The second, or southern, phase would begin with the capture of Sevastopol and the Crimea as well as the Kerch peninsula. This would clear the right flanks and permit an unhindered advance to Rostov and the gateway to the Caucasus. These pincers, one moving southward along the Don and another moving northward from the direction of Rostov, would then meet in the Stalingrad area so as to destroy all Soviet formations in the south and either capture the city or reduce its importance as an industrial center to insignificance. Once these operations had secured the northern and eastern flanks, operations into the Caucasus, code named '**Operation Edelweiss**,' could begin.

'Operation Edelweiss:' The German codeword for the invasion of the Caucasus region during 1942.

But before any operations could proceed the *Wehrmacht* needed to rebuild itself. During the period from June 1941 through March 1942 the Germans had suffered grievous losses: 1 100 000 killed, wounded, or captured, or nearly one-third of the entire invasion force in June 1941. The combat efficiency of Army Group Center, the largest of the armies, was at 65 per cent capacity due to its enormous losses (which could not be replaced). The losses were so severe all along the front that the rebuilding of the German army during the spring of 1942 had to rely upon a number of expedients and creative measures in order to be successful; Halder had not exaggerated German weaknesses at Orsha. These measures included replacing lost draught horses with animals seized from Soviet farmers, reducing all German divisions by about one-third and creating entirely new divisions from the 'surplus,' and removing most vehicles from the infantry divisions for reassignment to the motorized divisions. These measures were effective in improving the German fighting capacity, and by June 1942 64 per cent of all divisions (134 out of 209) were considered by OKH as 'capable of any offensive action' whereas only 5 per cent had been classified as such in March (8 out of 162). Since

Army Group South had the primary tasks for 1942 it received priority for replacements and rebuilding, receiving Fourth Panzer Army and a total of 20 infantry divisions (as well as 21 Hungarian, Italian, and Romanian divisions, whose task was the extremely important one of securing the flanks of the advancing Germans and clearing out enemy pockets surrounded by the Germans). As this force was accumulated, training exercises and planning continued for the successful implementation of the operation.

But the Soviets had their own agenda. Buoyed by their incredible successes at Moscow and elsewhere during the spring of 1942, *Stavka* envisioned a major operation to destroy Army Group South and imperil Army Group Center. Stalin was convinced that the Germans were teetering on the verge of collapse and he thought that a series of well-timed blows could, potentially, unhinge the entire German front and lead to Soviet victory in 1942. The plan which developed from these ideas was a blow against Army Group South in order to penetrate behind it, recapture Kharkov in grand encircling movements, and the destruction of the German forces in the south. This would then permit strategic operations against the belly of Army Group Center designed to destroy it as well. South of Kharkov the Soviets held a large bridgehead at Izium, while just north of the city they also held a smaller one. These would be, from the Soviet viewpoint, a perfect launching point for an envelopment of that vital industrial city and the unfolding of operations. Southwestern *Front* therefore concentrated large reserves in these areas, especially mobile forces and armor, to break through and rapidly develop pincers to reach around from the north and south and shut behind the German defenders around Kharkov. The attack would begin as soon as the spring rains, the *rasputitsa*, ended.

On 12 May the Soviet offensive began even though the rains had not yet quite subsided and the forces were not quite totally prepared (see Plate 6). Unfortunately for the Soviets, the Germans had planned to eliminate the Izium bridgehead as part of the early phases of 'Operation Blue,' beginning on 18 May. In order to halt the Soviet offensive all that was necessary was to launch their operation a few days early and, in effect, turn the Soviet successes into a deadly trap. Once the Germans began pressing their attack against the neck of the Izium bulge any movement westward by Soviet troops was a step into a cauldron and disaster. *Stavka* failed to recognize this and kept pressing the offensive until 20 May, but by 22 May the neck at Izium had been broken and the trap was closed; the Red Army lost about three rifle divisions and a tank army. This battle, the second battle for Kharkov, was a disaster for the Red Army but taught the *Wehrmacht* a lesson as well: while an outstanding victory, it had not come cheaply and was thus a 'modest victory' – it only mauled the Red Army, it did not annihilate it (Wegner, 2001). The German units involved in the battle had to be refitted and rested after their victory, and the Soviet offensive caused the delay of 'Operation Blue' until 28 June.

For the Soviets it was clear that their offensive, and the failure to end it once the Germans launched their counteroffensive, was a serious mistake. The forces lost in the battle could have been used in later operations and may have, potentially, slowed the German advance towards the Don and Volga rivers. Despite these failures, however, there was a positive note: after the battle Stalin and the top leadership were more likely to listen to their commanders in the field. The second battle for Kharkov was an operational failure, but the Soviets learned to be more realistic about their potentialities and tried to never again overreach themselves in such a way. (Glantz, 1998).

As the disaster at Kharkov unfolded Manstein and the Eleventh Army struck the Crimean *Front* as part of the clearing operations for 'Operation Blue.' An earlier Crimean offensive (February through April) by the Red Army had failed to dislodge the Germans from the peninsula despite heavy fighting and when Manstein struck on 8 May his units drove the exhausted Soviet armies into the Kerch peninsula, forcing them to leave behind a pocket of men protecting Sevastopol. The *Luftwaffe* began bombing Sevastopol in earnest as Manstein brought up enormous artillery pieces, including some of the largest guns ever made. The plan was for the combined air and land bombardment to reduce the city to rubble and kill most of its defenders; when the infantry entered the ruins costly house-to-house fighting could therefore be avoided. During the remainder of May and June the intense fighting and shelling continued to shrink slowly the area under Soviet control. By 4 July, after one of the most intensive bombardments of the war, the city was cleared of Soviet resistance. Despite the losses and time taken to complete the mission, Manstein was rewarded with promotion to field marshal. The twin victories at Kharkov and the Crimea, which cost the Red Army a great deal of men and materiel, were a relief for the German people and command structures after the almost continuous bad news from Moscow the previous winter.

While the victory at Kharkov was without doubt militarily useful, it is debatable whether the battle for the Crimea was necessary. Would it have served better purposes (and the limitations of German resources) to encircle and besiege the city (like Leningrad), or were the huge German losses worth the effort of seizing Sevastopol? Would the enormous resources spent on capturing this city, which had limited significance for the prosecution of the war, have been better spent capturing Leningrad, which was a cultural, political, and military center? Its main purpose seems to have been a propaganda victory to bolster confidence at home, encourage German allies, and provide Hitler and his top commanders with relief from the frustration of seeing all their plans fail. An entire army, which could have been used elsewhere, was thus preoccupied with a task whose primary goal was to convince public opinion that Germany was still winning the war. It was, in essence, a victory of prestige rather than a military one (Wegner, 2001).

By the end of June the preliminary operations had been successfully concluded and it seemed as if 'Operation Blue' would be off to an excellent start. But two episodes related to German intelligence agencies highlighted the grave dangers facing the Germans. On 28 June, the very day 'Blue' was launched, German army intelligence issued a report which recognized the 'modest' nature of the victories thus far (the Red Army had managed to avoid being encircled in most cases) and concluded that the impending operation would not destroy the Red Army (Wegner, 2001). The second intelligence event was a potentially devastating error on the part of a German staff officer. On 19 June a German plane crash-landed behind Soviet lines and the staff officer was captured carrying a detailed copy of the German plans. Stalin, fearing that the plans were a planted deception, refused to believe they were accurate and ignored them. The Germans, realizing that the Soviets could never be sure that the plans they captured were fake, took a calculated risk and decided to stick to the plan. On 28 June the offensive began in the north; the idea was to start the operation with a drive to Voronezh in order to fool the Soviets into thinking that the ultimate goal was Moscow, and as late as 5 July *Stavka* continued to believe that the German plan was to assault Moscow from the south.

Fourth Panzer and Second Armies drove eastward between Bryansk and Southwest *Fronts* towards Voronezh. By 7 July the panzers had linked up with Sixth Army near Voronezh, but the Soviets had withdrawn rather than stand to fight and the Germans found themselves capturing, for the first time in the war, relatively few prisoners. The whole point of operations in the northern sector was to destroy the Red Army units which could interfere with the southern sector, and even during the first days of fighting it was becoming clear this was not occurring. Hitler recognized the failure of operations and sacked Bock on 13 July, ostensibly for his conduct of the battle at Voronezh (Bock insisted on crossing the Don and taking the city while Hitler thought the best approach was to stay on the western bank), but in reality out of frustration with the lack of prisoners. The pincers then turned southward towards the area between the Chir and Donets rivers in order to trap Soviet forces in the south, but found themselves taking few prisoners. The lack of prisoners has led to operations in the north being called a 'blow into thin air' as the Red Army disengaged from the fighting and withdrew across the Don river (Wegner, 2001). Operations in the north thus achieved the conquest of large amounts of territory, but did not destroy Red Army units in large numbers.

Once Voronezh had been seized Army Group B pivoted southward along the river towards the area east of Rostov so as to encircle the Soviet defenders in the region. But supplies, especially fuel, ran short (due, at least in part, to the increased expenditures at Kharkov) and the armor's advance was relatively slow. This hesitation, combined with Soviet perceptions of the potential disaster facing them, permitted most of the Soviet formations to continue their withdrawal so that as Army Group B reached the area of Rostov and closed the trap they found only about 54 000 prisoners.

The capture of Rostov on 23 July marked the end of the first phase of operations. At this point Hitler decided to split the armored forces of Army Group A, which was to drive into the Caucasus, so that a portion went ahead with operations into the Caucasus and another portion was sent to assist Sixth Army, which had proceeded along the Don towards Stalingrad. This move was given top priority for supplies as the German effort split into two: one focal point aimed at the Caucasus (the ultimate goal of 'Blue') and a second at Stalingrad and the erection of a defensive barrier to protect Army Group A. Rather than adhering to the original plan and allowing Army Group B to fulfill its goals before Army Group A pursued its objectives, the army groups were sent at the same time in divergent directions. The splitting of the German effort for 'Operation Blue' has usually been seen as the cardinal error of the eastern campaign. It is a military maxim, as we have seen, to concentrate on single goals. Hitler, who by now was again confident of his abilities and victory, split the German effort into unrealizable goals; singly the *Wehrmacht* may have captured either Stalingrad or the Caucasus, but it could not safely do both. This, at least, was Halder's view; already on 26 July he had written that Hitler's insistence upon tactical victories rather than strategic ones was a policy which he was not sure would accomplish German goals (Halder, 1988: 487). The real difference between Halder's view (and FHO agreed with him) and Hitler's was that the former thought the Red Army, because it had not permitted itself to be drawn into battles of annihilation in the north, had not been destroyed and would continue to threaten the operation in the Caucasus and that therefore the *Wehrmacht* should continue its focus on the northern sector. Hitler, on the other hand, thought it was merely a matter of pursuing the already shattered Red Army beyond the Volga; Hitler now believed both phases of 'Blue' could be accomplished at once. The core of the argument between Halder and Hitler was, in essence, the army's insistence upon annihilating the enemy and Hitler's desire to achieve the economic goals of 'Blue.'

But the advance into the Caucasus did not go exactly as planned either. As the Germans moved southward they discovered that the precious oil fields had been destroyed by the withdrawing Red Army and could not be put back into production without major and lengthy repairs. Ironically, as Army Group A drove further from its supply railheads at Rostov into the oil-rich Caucasus the supply of oil products, as well as ammunition, became increasingly problematic. Compounding these difficulties was the geographical fact that as they drove southward the area of operations grew larger and the front correspondingly longer. Army Group A, in other words, found itself unable to man the front lines on its left flank in the Kalmyk Steppe and had to spread itself thinly along its remaining front the further it advanced. The lack of manpower slowed the German advance and permitted the Soviets to create fairly effective strong points which acted as further brakes upon the German progress.

On 22 July a series of violent attacks were made on First Panzer as it tried to break into the Caucasus. These attacks, while not preventing a breakthrough, certainly created enormous difficulties for the Germans. It was not until 29 July that the Germans were able to sever the last rail line exiting the Caucasus into the Soviet Union. The potential loss of access to the Caucasian oil fields created a panic in Moscow, and in anticipation of the impending break in oil deliveries *Stavka* issued Order Number 227, which decreed that no Soviet units were to retreat under any circumstances without suffering serious penalties. *Stavka* also created 'blocking units' which were to open fire, if necessary, to stop fleeing units [**Doc. 16, p. 119**]. This 'not a step back' order did not, of course, stop Soviet retreats when these were considered strategically or tactically necessary, but it did help to reduce panic retreats among Soviet units and put an end to the wholesale withdrawal of the previous weeks.

The eastward pace of Army Group B's operations slowed in early August as it stopped to hoard supplies and focus on its northern flanks along the Don. As it halted the focus shifted to Army Group A, which continued to advance towards Grozny, capturing Maikop on 9 August. But as its supply and front lines lengthened the Germans became considerably bogged down, and finally operations in the Caucasus were brought to a halt on 28 August, just short of Grozny. While this was in reality an operational failure and a signal that the main goals of 'Blue' had not been achieved, it was hailed as a success by German propaganda, especially the image of German military skiers planting a German flag on top of Mt Elbruz, the highest peak in the Caucasus mountains, about 100 miles west of Grozny.

Army Group B resumed its march eastward at almost the same time that Army Group A ran out of steam; on 23 August it crossed the Don and headed for Stalingrad. But the realization that things were not going according to plan led to a conference at Vinnitsa on 7 September. At this conference Hitler argued that the errors and mistakes thus far resulted from Field Marshal **Wilhelm List** not closely following orders, but Jodl countered that List had scrupulously followed all of Hitler's orders. The result of this disagreement was List's removal on 10 September and Hitler's continuing estrangement from his top commanders; henceforth stenographers were to record faithfully every word uttered during the conferences to ensure that Hitler's orders were followed to the letter. This meeting intensified the distrust between Halder and Hitler, strained since the operations at Moscow nearly a year before, and

List, Wilhelm (1880–1971): Commander of Army Group North during the initial invasion of the Soviet Union in 1941–42. He was dismissed from his post in 1942 and served in no other position during the war.

on 24 September he too was relieved of his position. Halder described this in his memoirs as the final crisis between his professionalism and Hitler's amateurism, but this explanation is too simplistic. Halder, it seems, broke with Hitler at this time because he realized he could no longer prevail in discussions with Hitler, that his 'professionalism' could no longer temper Hitler's optimism. Hitler would now, with or without Halder, commit such grave errors with the tattered *Wehrmacht* that it could never recover or win the war. He therefore believed that the war was lost at the same time that Hitler, while still optimistic that the war could be won, had begun to realize that the goals of 'Blue' could not be achieved in 1942. The operation was the brainchild of Hitler, who conceived it, ordered it, and then passed responsibility for making it happen to the army. But as operations failed to net the expected prisoners (which, it was thought, reflected the destruction of enemy formations), Hitler blamed his generals for their failure to execute faithfully his plans. The tension between the two men thus reached a breaking point as each realized the failure of operations yet again (Wegner, 2001).

As the advance into the Caucasus stalled Hitler shifted his focus towards Stalingrad. He sent armored and infantry reinforcements to Sixth Army to ensure that this target, at least, was neutralized so that the drive towards the oil fields could recommence and achieve its goals (see Plate 7). But the Soviet defenders were determined to hold the city, not just for prestige purposes but also as a magnet drawing the Germans into a trap. While **Vasily Chuikov**, the Soviet general responsible for the defense of Stalingrad, erected a tenacious defensive effort to prevent the Germans from taking the city and at the same time encourage them to send more units into the battle, *Stavka* was planning an offensive. The battle for Stalingrad, one of the most iconic of the war, was about to begin in earnest.

THE BATTLE FOR STALINGRAD

The Soviets massed, without a shred of German awareness, huge resources north and south of Stalingrad. In June 1942 **Alexander Vasilevsky** had become the head of the Soviet General Staff, and he and his subordinates, especially Zhukov and Timoshenko, began creating operational plans for the destruction of the German armies. Their plans, which husbanded resources even during the most dangerous times for Stalingrad, envisioned two attacks on the weak Romanian flanks. The penetration of these lines would create an opportunity for a classic double envelopment of the forces in the Stalingrad area by closing pincers behind their position. This concept, presented on 13 September, evolved into three operations: '**Operation Saturn**,' '**Operation Uranus**,' and '**Operation Mars**.' 'Uranus' was designed to cut off and destroy

Chuikov, Vasily (1900–1982): Soviet army commander responsible for the defense of Stalingrad. His forces also participated in the capture of Berlin in 1945 and he negotiated its surrender with the Germans.

Vasilevsky, Alexander (1895–1977): Member of the Soviet general staff and army commander responsible for many of the largest operations during the war, including Stalingrad, Kursk, the liberation of the Crimea, and 'Operation Bagration.'

'**Operation Saturn**:' The Soviet operation against Rostov to eliminate Army Group A in the Caucasus during the early winter of 1942. It was modified into 'Little Saturn' after the Germans launched a relief effort to save the Sixth Army in Stalingrad.

'**Operation Uranus**:' The Soviet codeword for the offensive against Army Group B which resulted in the encirclement at Stalingrad.

'**Operation Mars**:' The Soviet offensive against Army Group Center, November, 1942.

the Germans in Stalingrad, while 'Saturn' was to then push the rest of Army Groups A and B out of the eastern Ukraine. 'Operation Mars' was to be launched against Army Group Center and thus prevent it from sending reinforcements southward to assist Army Groups A and B. These operations would thus permit the Soviets to roll up the entire Eastern Front and destroy two army groups.

Nikolai Vatutin, in command of Southwestern *Front*, was to send mobile units through the armies of German allies north of Stalingrad and drive them to the region west of the city. Stalingrad *Front*, led by Yeremenko, would then drive through the Romanian armies south of the city and push for the same general area as Vatutin's forces. The two pincers were to meet in the area of Kalach, about 40 miles west of Stalingrad. In order to confuse the Germans and force them to commit their slender resources too early, the operations were to begin a day apart on 19 and 20 November.

The success of the operation depended upon the rapid collapse of the Romanian armies. The Germans realized the weak spot of the front was that held by their allies and 'corseted' them with German units, but these were themselves fairly weak. Part of the problem for the Romanians was that the Germans had not been able to keep their promises to better equip the Romanians with heavy weapons, especially anti-tank weapons. Since the Soviet forces were top-heavy with armor, the Romanian units were easily routed during the first day of fighting and 27 000 Romanians were taken prisoner. By 22 November the armored pincer from the north had reached Kalach and, through a bold ruse, captured an important bridge. During the next afternoon the southern pincer, also easily advancing against the Romanians, also reached Kalach and closed the trap around Stalingrad. The 330 000 Germans of Sixth Army were trapped.

Almost immediately (25 November) 'Operation Mars' began. The goal was to drive Kalinin and Western *Fronts* against the large salient left over from the battles for Moscow the previous year (called the Rzhev salient), pinch it off and prepare for operations further west against Smolensk. The concept was very similar to that of 'Uranus,' but Army Group Center was able to defeat this operation despite **Ivan Konev's** best efforts. This defeat was humiliating enough and such a contrast to the victories achieved in the south that the Soviets kept it secret for decades, refusing to even admit it had taken place (Glantz, 1999).

'Operation Saturn's' goal was to push part of Southwest *Front* past Italian units guarding the Don and drive southward to Rostov, thus cutting off Army Group A in the Caucasus. But a relief effort led by Manstein to break the ring around Stalingrad from the south prompted a change in plans. 'Little Saturn,' as it came to be called, began on 16 December and pounded the defenders on the Chir and Don rivers, virtually obliterating the entire Italian army.

Vatutin, Nikolai (1901–44): One of the most capable of Soviet generals, during the early days of the war he fought against Army Group North and helped blunt its advance towards Leningrad. He served alternately as front commander and representative of *Stavka* to the various fronts. He participated in the battles of Kursk, Kharkov, and the recapture of Kiev. He was killed by Ukrainian partisans in the spring of 1944.

Konev, Ivan (1897–1971): Soviet army commander who fought from the first days of June, 1941 in the area of Army Group Center. His armies launched the counterattack at Moscow in 1941 which stopped the Germans. He also took part in the battles of Kursk, Korsun, Kanev, Kharkov, and Berlin, which he is credited with capturing (also spelled Koniev).

Plate 1 A German police unit murders civilians in the Ukraine

Plate 2 The Massacre at Babi Yar, September 1941

Plate 3 A German unit commits mass murder

Plate 4 German vehicles in the mud, December 1942

Plate 5 Germans captured at Moscow, January 1942

Plate 6 Soviet tanks and infantry, May 1942

Plate 7 Germans in Stalingrad, November 1942

Plate 8 Germans in Kharkov, December 1942

Plate 9 Field Marshal Paulus surrenders at Stalingrad, February 1943

Plate 10 The victorious Soviet generals

Manstein's effort to relieve Stalingrad, begun on 12 December, now ran into serious difficulties both from the Red Army and Hitler, who refused to permit Sixth Army to exit the trap through the corridor Manstein was creating. He allowed the relief effort to continue, but forbade any westward movement through the corridor which resulted in the abandonment of Stalingrad, thus making a mockery of the effort to relieve Sixth Army. Paulus, in command of Sixth Army, refused to disobey orders and break out on his own authority, as Manstein suggested, and so the linkup between the relief column and Sixth Army never occurred. Strong Soviet pressure made it increasingly difficult to keep the corridor open and the relief effort was gradually brought to a halt by weather, intensive fighting, and Hitler's intransigence.

By 18–19 December everyone realized that there was no hope of saving Sixth Army. The Soviet offensive ('Little Saturn') combined with a lack of German resources meant that the relief effort could not be maintained. By this time most of the fighting was taking place about 100 miles west of the city as the defenders of 'Fortress Stalingrad' tenaciously maintained their grip on the city. The decision by Hitler to supply it by air was a total failure despite the promises made by an incompetent Göring, as the Germans lacked the machines necessary to carry it out and the Soviets created their first effective anti-aircraft barrier of the war. Food, fuel, and ammunition slowly dwindled and the men both starved and had to fire their weapons sparingly. As operations receded further west and the Soviet ring was tightened around the city, Sixth Army slowly died. On 24 January the last German airfield in the pocket fell to the Red Army as the Soviets constricted the ring around the city. Paulus maintained a steady litany of requests for supplies, but it was now impossible to fly these into the German positions. Hitler responded to the impending crisis by making Paulus a field marshal on 30 January, apparently because no German field marshal had ever been captured and Hitler hoped Paulus would follow precedent and commit suicide. It was pointless: by 31 January the German positions had been cut into two and Paulus surrendered his small pocket of men, permitting the other half to fight on if they chose to do so (see Plate 9). The last pocket surrendered on 3 February, and at last the drama was over: 90 000 men went into captivity; the vast majority of them never returned home.

As the Soviets carrying out 'Little Saturn' bore down on Rostov, Army Group A, deep in the Caucasus, was in serious trouble. All supplies for the army group ran through Rostov and to lose it meant a second Stalingrad and the virtual destruction of German forces in the south. Hitler, hesitant as always to withdraw even under pressure, finally ordered part of the Army Group to pull out through Rostov on 27 January, but a large portion remained behind in a bridgehead around the Kuban peninsula, where it remained (in Hitler's fertile imagination) as a possible launching pad for further attacks. In the weeks which followed the *fronts* all along the southern sector began offensives which pierced and penetrated ad hoc and shattered German units on the Mius and Chir rivers. For the Germans this was the most dangerous period of the war up to this point, even more so than during the battle for Moscow (Beevor, 1998).

GERMAN EFFORTS TO HALT THE RED ARMY

By the time Paulus was playing out the end of the sordid story in Stalingrad the front was far to the west (about 50 miles from Kharkov). Soviet operations continued to press the desperate Germans back from position after position, and it seemed as if the entire southern front would collapse from the pressure. During February the Red Army made significant gains in the Don river basin, an important industrial center. On 12 February 1943 Hitler combined Army Group Don (newly created after Army Group B had been surrounded) and Army Group A into Army Group South under Manstein. On 16 February he learned that Kharkov had been recaptured by the Soviets two days earlier and that they were rapidly advancing towards Dnepropetrovsk, the major supply node for the entire southern army group. Hitler therefore flew to meet Manstein in order to compel him to retake Kharkov at once. Manstein, however, had another idea: the Red Army was now hundreds of miles from its supply bases east of the Don, while his army group was literally in the lap of its railheads. He therefore proposed that a counteroffensive be launched to halt the Red Army before it reached the Dnepr and in the process recover Kharkov.

On 20 February the attack, which Hitler had approved, was launched and achieved great operational success due to Soviet over-extension and German fighting skills. The units threatening Dnepropetrovsk were halted and thrown back while Kharkov was retaken (the third battle for Kharkov) on 15 March (see Plate 8). The only reason the Soviets did not suffer another total disaster at Kharkov was that the onset of the *rasputitsa* caused a lull in the fighting.

Manstein's offensive brought a halt to the Soviet drive which had begun in November at Stalingrad. The massive disasters the Germans had suffered during the winter of 1942–43 were thus redeemed, at least psychologically, and Hitler began to prepare for a new summer campaign for 1943, the third of the war. It also humbled *Stavka*, which was forced to realize that the *Wehrmacht* remained, however crippled it appeared to be, a formidable opponent. By the end of 1942 Soviet casualties were over 11 000 000, but the incredible German advance had been blunted and losses far heavier than German planners had ever anticipated had been inflicted. Most importantly, however, the Soviet army had, as one scholar put it, 'learned to fight' (Glantz, 1991). This would be convincingly demonstrated during the German summer offensive of 1943.

The German summer offensive of 1942 had failed to achieve its goals and had turned, like the offensive of 1941, into a disaster. The lack of a main effort combined with battles of prestige to reduce the German offensive to nothing but an enormous waste of resources. The failure was thus one of planning and execution: a flawed plan was carried out in a manner (the division of effort in July) that virtually guaranteed almost insurmountable difficulties. The defensive line along the Volga, upon which so much relied for the safety of the advance further south, was an inherently indefensible line for the Germans as they could not keep it supplied or manned; it could not have been maintained even if the Soviet offensive had not broken it (Wegner, 2001). The failure of 'Operation Blue' was thus total: no oil fields were captured; the Donbas remained in Soviet hands; five German armies had either been destroyed or routed; none of the goals which German planners had set had been reached.

Was the battle of Stalingrad, which was so expensive in terms of human lives and materiel, worth the cost? With the failure of Army Group A, whose goals were after all the central point of 'Operation Blue,' the focus had shifted northward to Stalingrad. The capture of this city, which had little strategic value, became important as a prestige victory, as a banner which the Germans could wave to show they were winning the war. This was especially true once German news, bereft of other stories, began to focus on the fighting in the city. In this regard the battle became important psychologically, if not militarily. Hitler himself compounded this dilemma on 8 November 1942 when, in his annual speech to the party faithful, he declared that Germany would 'never leave Stalingrad.' But the battle might have been won had the Germans focused on military targets of high value rather than propaganda victories. One recent author has suggested that the Germans might have inflicted a crushing blow on the Soviet economy if Baku had received the aerial bombardment suffered by Stalingrad during August and September; 80 per cent of Soviet oil flowed through pipelines in this city (Hayward, 1998). Instead of reducing a strategically unimportant city to rubble it might have paid handsome dividends to reduce Baku to ruins; thus at least some of the strategic goals of 'Blue' might have been achieved.

Was Stalingrad a turning point in the war, or perhaps even the turning point? This suggests that had the Germans captured the city the war might have turned out differently, that its capture might have been a war-winning act. But the extreme inequality of resources between Germany and the Allies precludes any notion that Germany might have won the war even with the petroleum resources of the Caucasus. The Soviet victory at Stalingrad thus cannot be considered a turning point in the war as a whole. But can it be seen as a turning point in the war in the east? During both 1941 and 1942 the USSR came close to collapse, and after Stalingrad the Germans had no hopes of ever bringing the Soviets that close to defeat again, even by their own admission. The loss in 1942–43 meant that Germany would be incapable of exploiting strategic opportunities in the east, and it does therefore seem that the loss at Stalingrad marked a point after which there was no possibility for Germany to win the war in the east.

THE PARTISANS

As German fortunes on the southern part of the Eastern Front began to spiral out of control the partisan war in the center also began to increase in tempo and pace during 1942. The operations of the partisans, while small and generally unspectacular, were nonetheless grating on German patience. The partisan movement has acquired a halo of heroism and a panoply of legends surrounds them. Most of the early partisans were Red Army soldiers left behind Army Group Center as the Germans advanced; unable or unwilling to surrender or return to their units, they survived as best they could in the forests and swamps of the western USSR. In January 1942 there were an estimated 100 000 organized into hundreds of groups, but during the spring and summer of 1942 this number grew to around 150 000 because of German anti-partisan policies, Soviet policy towards partisans, and a change in attitude by Soviet civilians who saw in partisans a possible savior from the draconian German occupation policies: requisitions, collective punishment, and anti-Jewish genocide. In Belorussia, for example, a trio of Jewish brothers fled to the woods and organized an 'army' which harassed local Germans and managed to survive the war (Duffy, 2003). In May 1942 the USSR created the Central Staff of the Partisan Movement in order to coordinate the actions of the various groups and bring them under the control of *Stavka*. The Central Staff passed on orders, suppressed anti-communist partisans, and helped to meld the scattered groups into a relatively effective weapon until it was dissolved in January 1944.

The lack of sufficient forces for security enabled the partisan groups in some areas to cause considerable difficulties for the Germans. The official German estimate in January 1943 was that about 30 per cent of the rear area behind Army Group Center was 'pacified,' but in Belorussia specifically this fell to about 20 per cent (Wegner, 2001: 1010). Near Bryansk, for example, in June–July 1942 a 'partisan republic' was created which could field an army of about 10 000 men and controlled about 400 villages with a population of over 200 000. A German offensive finally destroyed it and scattered the partisans in July, but most of the forces survived (Wegner, 2001). Operations against the 'partisans' in fact commenced immediately after the invasion even though there was no organized partisan movement in 1941 (Shepherd, 2004). The executions by German army groups continued at a high rate until by May 1942 Army Group Center reported that it had killed 80 000 partisans at a loss of 1094 soldiers during the preceding month; the extreme inequality in the death toll suggests that the people killed were not well armed and thus probably not partisans but average villagers caught in the German net. This experience was a common one in the rear areas of Army Group Center.

Recent analysts have concluded that the partisan movement had a limited impact upon operations on the Eastern Front, and never clashed with or tied down army units on a regular basis, but in fact created an environment in which the Germans reacted to their attacks with an increasing crescendo of brutality against civilians. German partisan policy was radicalized by Stalin's speech of 3 July, when he called for active resistance behind the lines and this caused panic among German commanders because they knew they had not sufficiently pacified their rear areas (Shepherd, 2004). This policy, which essentially placed civilians between choosing the Germans or the Soviets, bred pragmatic decisions by villagers to either support or not support partisans based upon an assessment of the ability of the Germans to inflict harm locally (Wegner, 2001).

The policy in action has been described as it occurred during a raid in 1941: a unit 'ride[s] into [a village] at full speed and then out the other end, occupies the . . . village . . . and then gathers the whole village together . . . for inspection.' The commanding officers then decided upon the fate of the male inhabitants 'so that the area is cleared of opposition and pacified' (Birn, 1997: 278). This process was simply murder and recent research has shown that most of the villagers sorted out for murder were either Jewish or ordinary villagers, not partisans, and in 1941 the anti-partisan measures were really a cover for the mass murder of Jews (Birn, 1997). The reports of the *Einsatzgruppen* show this through the enormous discrepancy between the number of 'partisans' and Germans killed in battle, reporting the execution of 'partisans' whose real identity could only have been Jewish (Headland, 1992). The police battalions tasked with rear area security (and therefore coping with partisans) similarly murdered Jews as a matter of routine and an integral aspect of their duties (Westermann, 2005) [**Doc. 17, p. 120**].

The heart of the German concern with partisans was the plain fact that Germany had insufficient troops to both conquer and police the occupied territories. This meant that the few troops available for rear area security had to display, in the eyes of the *Wehrmacht*, absolute ruthlessness in order to prevent resistance from arising. Hitler said it best himself: the Germans need to 'shoot dead anyone who even looks at us askance' (Megargee, 2006). On 18 July 1942 an order was therefore issued which decreed that any armed formation found behind German lines, even if in Red Army uniform and clearly a Red Army unit, was to be classified as a guerilla unit and therefore shot on the spot. Five days later OKW officially decreed terror as the basis of anti-partisan warfare.

The anti-partisan measures taken by the army quickly became conflated with the policy towards Jews. Very early during the war German propaganda linked Jews and communism, describing communism as a tool by which Jews hoped to enslave mankind. Thus Jews were already identified as 'enemies' of the German army, hostile from the very beginning to German goals in the USSR. German security personnel therefore made periodic searches of POW camps culling any Communist party officials and Jews in order to shoot them. By 8 September the *Wehrmacht* gave the SS free rein to search POW camps for 'undesirables' for execution. On 7 October the army decreed the same, permitting the SS to remove anyone from the POW camps without explanation. Both Bock of Army Group Center and Rundstedt of Army Group South consented to this order (Megargee, 2006). A report of the SS for the end of July 1941 (a month into the invasion) reported that 6526 'Jewish plunderers' had been shot in Belorussia, clearly establishing that the link between Jews and 'enemies' existed from the early days of the war (Heer, 2000 (2)).

On 16 September 1941 OKH decreed that 50–100 communists would be shot for every German solider killed by partisans as a reprisal. The order to shoot guerillas on sight included anyone incapable of proving they had deserted; those who could not (and how, exactly, does one prove he is a deserter?) were shot. This applied to about one-half of all prisoners taken in the rear of Army Group Center during August and September 1941 (Heer, 2000 (2)). Being captured behind the lines meant almost certain death: of 10 940 prisoners taken in western Belorussia by mid-November 1941, 10 431 had been shot (Heer, 2000 (2): 97). In one operation behind Army Group Center during April 1942 2000 'partisans' were killed, but of these 1693 had been burned to death en masse in village buildings; these were clearly not partisans but ordinary villagers caught in the German net (Heer, 2000 (2): 109).

On 18 August 1942 the situation grew even worse when Hitler gave Himmler complete control in the areas behind the *Wehrmacht's* zone of control. After this point rear area security was defined and maintained exclusively by the SS. Himmler quickly redefined partisans as 'bandits' and the anti-partisan war was henceforth to be called 'anti-bandit' warfare. On 23 October he appointed **Eric von dem Bach Zelewski** as commissioner for

Bach Zelewski, Eric von dem (1899–1972): *SS* General and Police Leader, he was the chief of the anti-partisan units on the eastern front after July, 1943. He was also in command of crushing the Warsaw rising in the summer of 1944.

anti-bandit warfare in the east and anti-partisan operations began to increase in frequency and ferocity under his command. Bach Zelewski believed the key to success was constant and successive waves of ruthless operations against partisan bases; anti-partisan policy reached its peak on 26 October 1942, when Göring issued directives which designated either the shooting or hanging of all captured 'bandits,' including women. A month later a further order said that 'against women and children every available means is to be used as long as it leads to success' (Heer, 2000 (2): 114). Anyone suspected of being a partisan, regardless of sex or age, was to be murdered.

'OPERATION CITADEL'

In 1941 the Germans tried to execute a strategic campaign with military, ideological, and economic goals; it utterly failed. In 1942 the *Wehrmacht* tried to achieve economic goals which had long-term strategic goals; this too, failed miserably. By the spring of 1943 Germany desperately needed some kind of victory, not least in order to impress upon its allies that it was winning the war. Finland, Italy, and Hungary were all wavering in their support of German goals, and Turkey had already decided to stay out of the war. The problem was where to strike.

Manstein's successful offensive against the Soviets at Kharkov had not only stopped the Soviet steam-roller and restored the front-lines to some semblance of stability, it also created a large bulge around the city of Kursk. This salient provided a natural target for an encirclement by cutting it off at its eastern edges. This would have trapped two *fronts*, Central and Voronezh, and, the Germans hoped, wreaked such havoc upon the Red Army that no further activity could be expected from the Soviets that summer; the Germans could then recover and rest. It was, in essence, a defensive plan: the hope was to strike and prevent another series of offensives such as those after Stalingrad. The operation would also create a shorter front line and release about 20 divisions for other duties, including another offensive into the Caucasus.

Planning thus proceeded on what came to be called 'Operation Citadel.' The northern pincer, concentrated around Orel, would push south to meet a southern pincer coming from around Belgorod and seal a cauldron around all Soviet forces west of the juncture. The northern sector fell within the operational area of Army Group Center while the southern pincer fell within that of Army Group South, and this was the first multi-group operation since 'Barbarossa' two years earlier. The idea behind the operation was to preempt any potential Soviet offensive and so the Germans had to strike as soon as the *rasputitsa* ended; the original start date was 3 May. Part of the preparations

'Operation Citadel:' The German codeword for the offensive against the bulge at Kursk during the summer of 1943.

included having to rebuild most of the German units and the introduction of new weapons to overcome the materiel deficiencies. The infantry received a new light machine gun, the MG42, which permitted a far greater rate of fire than the bolt action Mauser rifles most soldiers carried. The panzer units began receiving new tanks too, the famous Tiger and Panther models. Both were vast improvements over the previous tanks available to the Germans, and while the Tiger proved to be a formidable weapon the Panther had been introduced before adequate testing and proved to suffer from crippling mechanical failures. The high command also began stripping other sectors of the front and rear areas of all available manpower, removing, for example, almost all of the combat divisions from France.

Kluge, Günther von (1882–1944): As Field Marshal, he participated in the invasion of France in 1940 and spent the rest of his career on the Eastern Front. He was in command of Army Group Center from 1943–43. In 1944, Kluge replaced Rundstedt as commander of the Western Front. He committed suicide in August 1944.

Army Group Center, under the command of **Günther von Kluge**, was to concentrate the Second Army and an infantry army, the Ninth, for its role in 'Citadel.' Ninth Army possessed large armored units and had about 1450 tanks and assault guns. The plan was for part of the armored units to launch the attack and blast a hole in the Soviet lines; the remainder of the armor would wait for five days for the full development of the breach and drive southward towards Kursk. Army Group South, under the command of Manstein, was to place the Fourth Panzer Army in the Belgorod area and then drive northward towards Kursk. The two armored pincers were to meet in the area east of Kursk by the fifth or sixth day of the operation and close the pocket, trapping all of the units of Central and Voronezh *fronts*. At the same time as the pincers were closing the trap Second Army, at the face of the bulge, would launch attacks to keep the Soviet defenders in place and prevent a large-scale withdrawal by the *fronts*. Second Army, like many other armies at the front, was worn out and heavily depleted from the fighting during the previous winter, and its role was simply to engage and hold the enemy in place and then assist in clearing the pocket of prisoners.

Model, Walther (1891 –1945): Panzer divisional commander in June 1941, subordinate to Guderian. Army commander in Army Group Center until January 1944 when he was given command of Army Group North, and then Army Group South when Manstein was relieved. In June 1944 he was given command of Army Group Center as it collapsed under the blows of 'Operation Bagration' (thus leading two Army Groups at the same time). In August 1944 he was transferred to France, and committed suicide rather than face capture.

The plan had its doubters and problems from the very beginning. On 30 April the start date was postponed because the *rasputitsa* had not yet ended. Manstein thought the German chance had therefore passed and that the Soviets were likely to launch an attack at any time. Guderian also argued that it was better to husband the tanks and vast resources gathered for 'Citadel' in order to better face the expected Soviet attack. Even Hitler voiced misgivings about the plan. **Walther Model**, commander of Ninth Army and a vital part of the operation, objected that Soviet defenses were simply too powerful and that expectations of a breakthrough on his part were most likely illusory. On 3 May these commanders met with Hitler and during a three day conference resolved nothing, not even a new start date. Further postponements were caused by a desire to increase the number of new Tigers and Panthers available for the panzer units, but ultimately, the order was given on 1 July for operations to begin on 5 July.

But by this time the Germans had given the Soviets more than two months to prepare, and time is one resource the Soviets rarely wasted. Just as in previous years, the Soviets hoped to launch a major offensive against the Germans in order to destroy their forces in the USSR. In formulating their plans for 1943, they determined that the most likely place for a German offensive was against the Kursk salient, as its reduction provided obvious benefits to the German army (such as releasing divisions for use elsewhere). Soviet reconnaissance confirmed these suspicions, and *Stavka* began to formulate its plans around this fact. Zhukov and Vasilevsky argued that the Red Army should prepare defensive positions around Kursk, permit the Germans to strike and then wear them down in a costly defensive battle. Once their fighting power had been eroded, Zhukov counseled launching a series of powerful offensives all along the German front. On 12 April at a meeting between Stalin, Zhukov, Vasilevsky, and other commanders the plan was accepted. Vasilevsky ordered the armies around Kursk to erect powerful anti-tank defenses and to step up intelligence gathering in order to determine exactly where the Germans could be expected.

Voronezh (commanded by Vatutin) and Central (commanded by Rokossovsky) *Fronts* were ordered to build formidable defenses and wage intensive defensive warfare. Their task was to engage and wear down the German attackers in order to force them to spend their energies trying to break through the Soviet lines. Bryansk and Western *Fronts* were to protect the northern flanks while Southwestern *Front* protected the southern flanks. The most important *front*, however, was a new one completely undetected by German intelligence: Steppe *Front* (commanded by Konev), located far behind the lines and held in reserve. Its job was to launch the Soviet counter-offensive once the Germans had been exhausted.

During the German pause before launching 'Citadel' the Soviets concentrated on building defensive works and replenishing their units with men and equipment. The T-34 was sent to the *fronts* in enormous numbers, and by the time 'Citadel' began there were over 20 000 Soviet tanks of all types in the region. Conscription and training increased the number of Red Army soldiers in just Central and Voronezh *Fronts* to 1 337 000 despite the enormous losses of 1941 and 1942.

The Soviet plan was for the massive defensive works to serve as a break-water upon which the German offensive would break to pieces. Once the Germans were stopped the Soviet *fronts* were to launch two major offensives: '**Operation Kutuzov**' towards Orel in the north and '**Operation Rumiantsev**' towards Kharkov in the south. The defensive lines consisted of a series of belts arranged thickly for many miles beyond the front, consisting of anti-tank ditches, machine gun nests, and traps engineered to force both tanks and men into a mass of minefields. The first zone, of two belts, consisted of

'Operation Kutuzov:' The Soviet operation against the northern neck of the Kursk bulge during the summer of 1943.

'Operation Rumiantsev:' The Soviet offensive against the southern neck of the Kursk bulge during the summer of 1943.

three trench systems, anti-tank minefields, and artillery placements each about one and one-half miles deep. The layout provided for a systematic employment of elastic defense, which allowed the depth of the defenses to slow and thin the ranks of the attackers until they reached an area in the bowels of the network where counterattacks could be launched against a depleted enemy (Glantz and House, 1999).

A second series of belts, a few miles beyond the first, was designed to stop any Germans who had penetrated beyond the first zone. A liberal use of mines with a density of about 2700 anti-personnel and 2400 anti-tank mines per mile channeled both men and tanks towards prepared anti-tank and machine-gun positions. This belt fronted another belt, which fronted another, for a total of eight defensive zones stretching more than 100 miles into the rear. The Soviets had turned the salient into a vast killing field backed by an entire *front* whose forces were to remain uncommitted until the enemy had been exhausted trying to fight through this net.

Late on 4 July a patrol from Rokossovsky's *front* captured a German clearing a path through a minefield. Interrogation revealed that the Germans would attack at 0330 that night, 5 July, so Rokossovsky ordered a massive artillery bombardment all along the northern edge of the salient near Ponyri in order to disrupt German preparations. The bombardment caught Ninth Army by surprise and delayed German preparations for an hour, but at 0430 German artillery finally answered back. By 0530 German infantry began to advance and ran immediately into the first defensive zone. Fierce fighting throughout the day saw the Germans advance about six miles into the first belt, but at a great price in men and equipment. Ninth Army thus launched the northern pincer amid heavy and hard fighting (see Map 4).

On the southern edge of the salient Fourth Panzer Army prepared to launch its offensive at the same time. Vatutin, however, also obtained information about the imminent attack and, like Rokossovsky, fired off an enormous artillery barrage on the assembling Germans at 0230. At 0330 the Germans began firing back with one of the largest German artillery barrages of the entire war. One-half an hour later Fourth Panzer begin the attack but ran into difficulties almost immediately. Within a few hours the attacks stalled as dozens of Panthers had been disabled by minefields as well as mechanical breakdowns. In most places the Germans enjoyed a minimum of success, and even broke through a few Soviet positions. But because of the tenacious and well-planned defensive systems the pace was well below what the plan required. In order to overcome these difficulties, the commander of Fourth Panzer, Hoth, decided to launch an attack which he thought would both confuse the Soviets and permit him to destroy their armored reserves (which he feared would otherwise strike his right flank as he advanced towards Kursk). He deployed his armor, II SS Panzer Corps, on a trajectory towards the village of Prokhorovka, a direction the Soviets did not anticipate because it lies on an axis further east of Kursk. He hoped to lure Soviet armor into a clash and once these had been destroyed or neutralized resume a northwesterly advance on Kursk. By the end of the first day Hoth's units had advanced about 11 miles into the defensive zone, and much of the credit for his success can be attributed to the *Luftwaffe*, which provided excellent ground support for his panzers. But despite the very high losses he was suffering, Hoth felt confident that the offensive could achieve its goals over the next several days.

Operational Group Kempf, whose task was to engage and destroy the Soviet armor in the south, had a much harder time than Hoth's forces. It was to move towards Korocha, defeat the enemy armor, and then move towards Prokhorovka to support Hoth. But stiff Soviet resistance kept it very close to its initial start position along the Donets river, preventing Kempf from fulfilling its part of the first day's mission.

On the second day of the German offensive Model began to press towards Olkhovatka and a nearby prominent hill, exactly as Rokossovsky predicted. The Soviets had already foreseen the importance of this area and had erected extremely tough defensive works and heavily fortified the area. Model was, in fact, heading for the most heavily fortified area in the entire salient. The anti-tank weapons, tank traps, and extensive minefields wreaked havoc among the German panzers and by the end of 6 July the Germans had not reached even the goals for the first day of operations. Over the next two days Model tried again and again to penetrate the defensive zone and each time failed at a heavy cost. The same story occurred at Ponyri: for six days the panzers tried relentlessly to break through and for six days utterly failed. Model fed in several infantry and panzer divisions in order to take the small village, hoping the sheer weight of manpower would break Soviet resistance. But this merely resulted in extremely high casualties and an unacceptable rate of loss of heavy equipment.

Model was thus unintentionally making the Soviet plan of bleeding the Germans a reality. He continued to send armor to attack strong points rather than maneuvering around them, and while in some cases this technique worked and the panzers were able to break through, the losses were staggering. By 9 July the furthest point of the German advance in the northern sector had been reached; after that day Model's forces lacked the forces to accomplish their mission.

In the southern sector the attack had gone more favorably and II SS Panzer Corps was ready by 6 July to attack the second defensive zone. By the end of that day elements had penetrated this second line near Luchki, but at such a heavy cost that the advance slowed to a crawl. On 7 July the Soviet lines were again pierced by panzer units and after heavy fighting the Red

Army began a disorderly and confused withdrawal towards the last major defensive belt in front of Oboyan. Elements of a panzer division even cut the road from Belgorod to Kursk for a time, while II SS Panzer Corps broke through and captured large numbers of Soviet prisoners. It looked as if Oboyan, which was about halfway to Kursk, would probably fall to the Germans. The Soviet command structure then issued orders to shore up its positions and prevent a German breakthrough. Vatutin fed armor and infantry into the lines, but on 8 July the panzers maintained their pace of operations towards Oboyan. By late on 9 July Fourth Panzer was only about 12 miles south of Oboyan but had lost, for the effort, 230 tanks and over 11 000 dead.

Operational Group Kempf had, in the meantime, taken steps which would prove to be of critical significance. Korocha was too well defended to be safely assaulted, so Kempf shifted westward toward Prokhorovka earlier than originally anticipated. This shift in emphasis meant that a mass of German and Soviet tank forces were heading for the same small village and were setting the stage for the largest tank battle in history.

On 10 July Model committed the last reserves of Ninth Army to a renewed assault upon Ponyri, thus eliminating any German forces which could be called upon in an emergency in the northern sector. This mistake meshed perfectly with the plans of *Stavka*, which had decided to launch Bryansk *Front* and the left flank of Western *Front* against the Orel bulge on 12 July ('Operation Kutuzov'). This attack would force Ninth Army to halt in order not to fall into a trap as the Soviets drove into the German rear. But Model's attack ran into such serious difficulties, despite reinforcements, that he put the entire Ninth Army, except those at Ponyri, on the defensive. Model thus curtailed the operations of the northen pincer after having advanced only six miles in five days of heavy fighting while suffering stupendous losses. A recent biographer of Model has analyzed why Ninth Army failed so miserably and at such a high cost, and part of the answer lies in the weakness of his formations before 'Citadel' began. It appears that on 5 July Model placed all of his available infantry in the trenches; the high casualties they suffered left him with insufficient forces to accomplish his mission. While lacking men, Model had sufficient armor and decided to devote it to the attack, bereft of infantry support, on 6 July; he thought he could better afford to lose tanks than infantry. But the tanks went into battle without the protective cover of infantrymen and then suffered correspondingly large losses themselves. His infantry divisions had suffered over 13 000 casualties from a force of 64 747 troops by 9 July and such a high rate of attrition was unsustainable given that the divisions were under strength and did not have the authorized number of men. Model therefore had at his disposal an infantry force incapable of achieving its goals given the formidable defensive barrier created by the Soviets (Newton, 2006).

10 July was also a significant day in the southern sector, but for different reasons. Hoth had sent a division to seize a bridgehead across the Psel river south of Oboyan; this position would permit the Germans to move into the rear areas of the Soviet formations and then race for Kursk virtually unopposed. This threat, and the movement of Operational Group Kempf towards the northwest, was so serious that Vatutin had to delay the planned offensive for 12 July in order to counter it. But despite the apparent German tactical successes in the south, it was clear that time was running out for the Germans strategically: on the same day (10 July) the Allies landed in Sicily. This forced OKH to transfer units from operations in the USSR to Italy and therefore weakened the German effort; the global war was beginning to impinge upon German capabilities even when they were successful.

On 11 July Army Group South launched its attacks on Soviet armor near Prokhorovka. Operational Group Kempf broke through defensive lines south of the village and began driving towards it while III Panzer Corps also converged upon it from the west. A desperate battle ensued for control of the approaches to the village in which newly arrived German forces were thrown straight into battle with entrenched Soviet forces. As nearly 900 German tanks converged on the site from two different directions, Vatutin tried to prevent their convergence through an immediate attack on the panzer forces at Prokhorovka to commence on 12 July.

At 0830 an intense artillery barrage opened the attack, quickly followed by 500 Soviet tanks. They moved in closely to the German vehicles and fired, in many cases, virtually at point-blank range. The tank battle degenerated into a confusing mass of tanks amid the cacophony of battle, made worse by the aerial battles going on overhead. As the day wore on it became increasingly clear that the Germans had not succeeded, and by the end of the day the arrival of III Panzer Corps had been prevented. The failure to mass their tanks in one place gradually told against the German effort, and more than 700 destroyed tanks from both sides littered the battlefield. The German offensive in the south, once so promising, had been stopped. Even Hitler had to face the reality of defeat and on 13 July suspended 'Citadel' after a week. Yet another major German offensive had failed.

But the Soviets were just getting started. On 12 July 'Operation Kutuzov' began against the Orel bulge in the north. **Ivan Bagramyan**, the commander of the Soviet Eleventh Guards Army in Western *Front*, had concentrated nearly all of his forces in a 10 mile sector facing Second Panzer Army. His goal was to push through the German lines and drive southward to meet elements of Bryansk *Front*, thus destroying Second Panzer and threatening

Bagramyan, Ivan (1897 –1982): Soviet general who was one of the planners of the failed offensive to recapture Kharkov in 1942, one of the primary generals at Kursk, and was instrumental in the offensives after 'Operation Bagration,' especially in pinning Army Group North into the Courland and effectively destroying it.

Ninth Army as well. The Germans, busy with trying to make 'Citadel' succeed, failed to notice the arrival of powerful forces opposite Orel and were taken by surprise. As the Soviets advanced Rokossovsky launched Thirteenth Army against Ninth Army and towards Orel, threatening the entire German position east of Bryansk.

At the southern neck of the Kursk salient the Germans kept pressure on the Soviet positions, and even managed to destroy several units on 15 July. But events elsewhere made these tactical victories of no consequence. On 17 July a Soviet offensive opened in the far south by Southwestern *Front* towards Kharkov. Model, in the north, was facing the near collapse of Ninth Army and was forced to conduct a withdrawal to a defensive line along the western edge of the Orel bulge, called the Hagen Line. These pressures forced OKH to withdraw units from Fourth Panzer Army in order to bolster Ninth Army and German forces in Sicily, and Fourth Panzer therefore found it necessary to surrender voluntarily the gains it had made during 'Citadel' as it no longer had the forces required to defend them; it pulled back to the start line as of 5 July.

On 3 August the second Soviet offensive, 'Operation Rumiantsev,' was launched at the southern neck of the Kursk salient. Voronezh and Steppe *Fronts* now had their chance to rip the German defenses to shreds. Belgorod was taken on 5 August, while in the north Orel was taken the same day. As the front collapsed all along the Kursk salient, Hitler ordered the building of a 'western wall,' a series of defensive points along the Dnepr over 100 miles behind the fighting. But this did not save the German forces fighting further east. The Soviet armies had taken a path which ran between Fourth Panzer and Operational Group Kempf, forcing them to withdraw. Kharkov was recaptured by the Soviets after a long and hard fight on 23 August (the fourth and last battle for the city). Konev and Vatutin managed, by capturing Kharkov, to eliminate the southern neck of the Kursk bulge. The salient was also straightened in the north on the same day with the elimination of the Orel bulge. The Red Army was by now approaching the German defensive line known as the Hagen Line, which had been hastily prepared just east of Bryansk.

The battle for Kursk has often been seen as a major turning point in the war, perhaps even the turning point. But like the battle for Stalingrad, this would imply that German chances for victory were somehow altered after the battle; that it represented a watershed after which it became impossible to win in the east. Part of this view relies upon the enormous casualties in both men and armor. The tank battle at Prokhorovka is said to have bled the German armor to a point beyond recovery. Recent research, however, tends to downplay German tank losses at Kursk. Soviet losses are put at around 70 000 men and 1600 tanks, while German losses are now estimated at

57 000 men and about 300 tanks (Mawdsley, 2005: 267). While these are enormous losses, especially for the Germans, they were not crippling. German strategic capabilities and opportunities were already limited before 'Citadel' (and its conception reinforced these limitations) so its failure (the third operational failure in three years) was not decisive.

What seems most significant about Kursk is not the German offensive, upon which so much scholarly effort has focused, but rather the Soviet offensives which both ended and followed it. The Soviets consider 'Operation Rumiantsev' their first battle of deep operations and thus the first modern battle of the war. This operation and its northern counterpart represented the culmination of Soviet experimentation in battle, particularly with mobile forces and the massive use of artillery. Kursk therefore represents the point at which the Soviets had managed to put together an effective offensive which both blunted and annihilated a German offensive (Glantz, 1991). Nonetheless, both 'Kutuzov' and 'Rumiantsev' failed to achieve the massive encirclements envisioned because the Germans withdrew in time; but these operations were still able to dislocate and fracture the entire southern and central sector of the German front.

The goal of 'Citadel' was never to strike the blow which would win the war, but to buy time for the Germans. The failure to obtain this time, signified not just by the reverses suffered at Kursk but also by the invasion of Sicily, was symptomatic that the tide had turned against the Germans long before 'Citadel' began. The battle for Kursk was therefore not as much a turning point as the signal that German hopes for victory had diminished beyond redemption.

4

The Soviet Union on the Offensive

BATTLES FOR THE UKRAINE

With the completion of operations 'Kutuzov' and 'Rumiantsev' during the late summer of 1943, the Red Army had been on the offensive, with a few brief respites because of the weather and the defensive battles at Kursk, since the previous November. Victories at Stalingrad, in the Ukraine, and Kursk had pushed the Germans back hundreds of miles from what would be their furthest advance into the USSR. But Soviet offensive plans were by no means exhausted, and the completion of the offensives related to the Kursk battles saw the eruption of a series of powerful and well-planned blows landed all along the German front, especially against Army Group South.

The Izium and Mius operations, launched in mid-July, were mainly designed to prevent the Germans from shifting forces from quiet regions to Kursk during the fighting in the salient. A third and more ambitious offensive in the far south, designed to recover the resource-rich Donbas region, crumpled German resistance. On 30 August Taganrog, the German anchor on the Mius after the loss of Rostov, was captured by the Soviets. The southern German line broke apart as *Wehrmacht* units fled westward closely pursued by the Red Army. Stalino was recaptured on 8 September as the Germans continued to race for the protection of the Dnepr river, which was reached at Zaporozhye on 22 September. This was an advance by the Red Army (and a corresponding German retreat) of about 200 miles in about three weeks and the signal that Army Group South, battered nearly to pieces after Stalingrad, was incapable of meeting the Soviet threat.

During the same time period (August–September) operations in the north kept the pressure on Army Group North but made little progress, while operations against Army Group Center, especially 'Operation Suvorov' by Kalinin and West *Fronts*, made significant progress. Launched on 7 August, 'Suvorov' was designed to push the Germans out of Russia and into

Belorussia, and on 25 September Smolensk was captured by the Soviets. In order to prevent the destruction of his army group Kluge was permitted to withdraw to defensive positions anchored on the upper Dnepr. In the far south the last Germans were expelled from the Kuban bridgehead in the Caucasus by early October, with Novorossiysk (the last major city in the Caucasus occupied by the Germans) taken on 16 September. Thus by the end of the summer of 1943 the Germans were retreating and on the defensive all along the Eastern Front. The most important aspect of the Soviet offensives of 1943 was that, even though still suffering disproportionately large losses, the Red Army was becoming a much more effective organization. Coordination of multi-*front* operations was proving to be much better handled than in February 1942, when disaster struck at Kharkov, and achieved much more impressive results. The Germans had not been encircled and annihilated as planned, but the Red Army was learning and losing less often than before. And it had major plans for the Ukraine during the remainder of 1943.

The Dnepr is a formidable barrier along much of its course: its western bank can rise over the eastern approaches as much as 100 feet and the river is up to 1000 yards wide. Prepared defensive positions along its western banks would have been virtually impregnable and everyone, from common foot soldiers to commanders, knew this. On 12 August Hitler suggested the creation of a defensive line running from the Sea of Azov to the Gulf of Finland, about 1000 miles long. Anchored on the Dnepr, it ran from Melitopol to Zaporozhye, then along the river to Lake Peipus and the sea. The southern segment was called 'Wotan,' the northern 'Panther.' In response to the stupendous attacks of the Red Army during the summer Hitler agreed on 15 September that the formations of Army Groups Center and South could withdraw to this line. Otherwise, both groups faced virtual destruction.

German soldiers hoped to shelter from the storm of steel which had been falling upon them all summer and very quickly the German retreat to 'Wotan' turned into a chaotic scramble [**Doc. 18, p. 121**]. But both 'Wotan' and 'Panther' were largely a figment of the imagination: under Hitler's orders virtually nothing had been built in order to ensure that it would not serve 'as a magnet' for the soldiers drawing them to its protection before the situation required them to pull back. The Germans therefore turned out to be just as vulnerable on the 'Wotan' line as they had been further east, with the sole exception (and an important one) of the difficulties the Red Army would experience crossing such a major river under fire.

As the Soviet *fronts* advanced across the Ukraine the *Stavka* decided to give them more geographically descriptive names, and so on 20 October they were renamed the First, Second, Third, and Fourth Ukrainian *Fronts*. The first blow by these *fronts* was the operation to retake Kharkov, launched on 3 August. The next major operation was the Chernigov–Poltava operation by Konev, Vatutin, and Rokossovsky. Fought in the same area which had seen the great encirclement battle by the Germans at Kiev three years earlier, it pushed the Germans back to the Dnepr near Kiev by the end of September. Further south Soviet troops crossed the Dnepr near Cherkassy and expanded a bridgehead as far south as Zaporozhye, a front about 175 miles long. The 'Wotan' line was also pierced by Fourth Ukrainian between Melitopol and Zaporozhye, which then drove quickly for the Dnepr at Kherson, about 100 miles from Odessa. This advance cut off the German Seventeenth Army in the Crimea, leaving it isolated and unable to contribute to the main battle. This advance also placed German occupation of the vital mines at Krivoy Rog and Nikopol in serious danger.

A massive airborne assault at Kanev, south of Kiev, on 23–26 September, whose purpose was to pierce the central portion of 'Wotan' initially ran into serious difficulties, but Vatutin shifted resources to the north of Kiev and by 3 November these broke across the Dnepr and recaptured Kiev on 6 November. With the recapture of Kiev, 'Wotan' was irreparably broken and Hoth, who had been responsible for the defense of Kiev, was relieved of command for losing the city and thus breaking the German defensive system. Vatutin, in the meantime, used these conquests to launch the Zhitomir–Berdichev operation, whose success created a salient north of the German positions and presented a threat of encirclement. Konev's *front* turned north from Kirovograd and met Vatutin's units, which had turned southward from their position near Kiev, trapping six German divisions. A relief effort by Manstein tried to break the men out of the pocket, but the snow, cold, ice, and powerful Soviet forces prevented him from opening a passage to the trapped men. Small German units were able, however, to filter through the Soviet lines and ultimately about 30 000 men escaped, though without their heavy equipment or wounded. About 18 000 Germans were captured.

Vatutin used these conquests as a springboard to the western Ukraine: on 24 December he commenced a new operation by driving southwest, taking Lutsk and Rovno on 2 February and entering the pre-war boundaries of Poland. Near Rovno Vatutin was ambushed by Ukrainian nationalists and severely wounded in an ensuing skirmish; he died in April. But First Ukrainian *Front* continued its advance and severed the last German rail line out of the Ukraine at Mogilev-Podolski, on 19 March, and as Zhukov took command it drove hard for the Carpathian mountains, capturing Chernovsty on 29 March. A final push put it over the Pruth river and into Romania by 7 April. Odessa, the last major city in the Ukraine still held by the Germans, held out until 10 April. By early April 1944 the non-stop Soviet offensives had freed the Ukraine from its German occupiers.

With the arrival of the Red Army in Romania the supply routes had finally been over-stretched and with the arrival of the *rasputitsa* the southern sector settled into a month of relative quiet. But Hitler, ever vigilant to find people to blame for the failure of his plans, decided on 30 March to retire forcibly both Manstein and Kleist; neither man was assigned another command during the war. Manstein has been called the best general who served during the war, and there is no doubt that he was, overall, superior to most of his colleagues. But his military prowess had been greatly exaggerated thanks to his brilliant conceptualization of the invasion through the Ardennes in 1940 and the operation at Kharkov in early 1943. The siege of Sevastopol, on the other hand, was hardly an inspiring example of military tactics as it tied down vast resources for an extended period of time in order to capture a city of dubious military value; it was more an example that brute force can capture objectives than careful planning or innovative tactics. The withdrawal from the Ukraine, over which he presided, was unprecedented in German military history and cost an enormous amount of men, materiel, and a precipitous drop in German morale. His military achievements after Kursk seem restricted to coping with one crisis after another, none very successfully. He was very interested in promoting the view of himself as a military strategist, and his post-war memoirs present a view of him and the *Wehrmacht* which deliberately distorts the behavior of the army on the Eastern Front. Any and all atrocities which occurred he blamed on the *SS* and he was therefore instrumental in the creation of the 'clean hands' myth of the *Wehrmacht*.

With or without Manstein, Hitler's main strategic conception after Kursk (the last German offensive in the east) was simply to hold on to all territory at all costs. To facilitate the recovery of territory lost to the advancing Red Army, Hitler decreed on 8 March 1944 that certain localities would be declared 'fortified places' in order to create a viable defensive system. These cities would permit themselves to be overrun and would then serve as a breakwater against which the Red Army would founder; a counterattack from these 'forts' would then restore German control over the entire area [**Doc. 19, p. 122**]. This order and Hitler's general refusal to permit withdrawals until it was too late to do so safely signified that Germany had run out of viable options by the end of the summer, 1943. Manstein had hoped to withdraw to the Dnepr defensive line, create reserves, and then, just as in February–March 1943, strike a powerful and decisive blow to stop the Red Army in its tracks. But six months after the remarkable victory at Kharkov this was, as Kursk had shown, simply wishful thinking. The *Wehrmacht* lacked the resources to conduct the kind of operations envisioned by Manstein while the Red Army was at the same time gradually beginning to outclass and outgun the Germans. The battle for the Ukraine marked a type of battle that would be repeated for the remainder of the war: sequential offensives all along the Eastern Front to force the Germans to react piecemeal and drain their resources rather than concentrating them; the goal was to evict the Germans from the USSR and take the war to Germany. Integral to this change was not just better coordination between Soviet forces, but the use of massed armor (and very few of these tanks were inferior to the German tanks), massed artillery (which vastly outnumbered the guns available to the Germans), and massed infantry.

During the height of the Ukrainian battles the Soviets launched several offensives to recapture the Crimea. At the end of October an amphibious landing at the straits near Kerch surprised the Germans, who nonetheless managed to put up a robust defense which delayed Soviet progress. Yeremenko and elements of Fourth Ukrainian *Front* were able to overcome these stumbling blocks and rather quickly captured Sevastopol and 21 000 German prisoners on 9 May, effecting a much quicker victory than Manstein and at a much lower cost (about 18 000 casualties of 450 000). By May 1944 the Germans had been evicted from the southern sector of the USSR.

THE RELIEF OF LENINGRAD

The Soviets were also very active in the north, launching the Leningrad–Novgorod operation on 14 January 1944 with the goal of lifting the siege of Leningrad and destroying Army Group North. The three *fronts* assigned the task, Second Baltic, Volkhov, and Leningrad with over 125 000 men and 1500 tanks, outnumbered Georg von Küchler's Army Group North by about 2–1 in men and 4–1 in tanks. The Army Group had, after Hitler ordered the building of the East Wall, erected its part of the Panther Line from Narva to Pskov and then southward to the positions of Army Group Center. During the fall the Soviet planners had expected the Army Group to follow the lead of the other German Army Groups and pull back to this line, but by early January the Germans had not retreated and Leningrad remained surrounded (a thin lifeline ran through Schlusselburg on Lake Lagoda).

The attack on 14 January came as a complete surprise to the Germans. Soviet pincers closed near Krasnoye Selo, capturing many of the German heavy guns which had been shelling Leningrad for two years. With this success German forces east of Leningrad were dangerously exposed and so they were withdrawn to the Luga river. As they withdrew the siege of Leningrad was completely lifted and the city once again had an open lifeline to the rest of the USSR for the first time in over 900 days. As the Germans withdrew they were closely followed by the Sixty-seventh Army, while at Novgorod Soviet pincers cut off another German pocket by 20 January. The entire front of Army Group North was reeling from the heavy blows and to prevent disaster Küchler asked for reinforcements and permission to fall back to the

'Panther' line at Narva-Pskov. But the American landings at Anzio on 22 January complicated the transfer of reinforcements to the Leningrad area and Hitler refused to give permission to fall back upon the 'Panther' line. As the Army Group faced one crisis after another its commander was replaced by Model on 29 January.

But Model, who was considered Hitler's 'fireman,' could not stop the Soviets either. On 12 February the city of Luga, a crucial railway junction and a key part of the defensive line, fell to the Soviets. Hitler now realized the crisis was acute and gave Model permission to pull back to the 'Panther' line at Narva, which held despite concentrated Soviet attacks which began on 9 March and continued through 15 April. But the Soviets had in the meantime turned southward, taking Pskov and reaching Ostrov by 1 March. But by this time the Soviet offensive had run out of steam amidst stout German resistance and by April 1944 a period of relative quiet settled along the entire eastern front thanks to exhaustion on both sides and the *rasputitsa*. The offensives which had begun with the battle at Kursk had finally run their course and in the process had driven the Germans from the Ukraine, relieved Leningrad, and caused innumerable losses which the Germans could not replace.

'OPERATION BAGRATION'

The *rasputitsa* season of spring 1944 saw a gradual slowing of operations all across the front. The winter operations of 1943–44, following the success at Kursk, had proven that the Red Army could defeat the *Wehrmacht*, although at great cost. The Germans had no hope of opening another summer offensive in 1944; the lack of resources and men was simply far too great. The Germans knew that the Red Army would launch its own offensive once the muddy season ended, but the question was where the attack would come. The incredible Soviet successes in the Ukraine and the relatively open terrain there suggested that operations might continue in that region as these offered the strategic opportunity of a giant encircling maneuver towards the north to cut off Army Groups Center and North. In addition, repeated efforts by the Soviets to dislodge Army Group Center since early 1942 had failed, so the German high command felt confident that any offensive in that region could be contained. Army Group North's line was also holding despite repeated Soviet attempts to break it. Hitler therefore believed the Soviets would follow their success and attack into the northern Ukraine.

This assessment, although sound if German assumptions are accepted, was seriously misinformed. The Soviets in fact intended to smash through the center of the German front, push as far west as possible, and then launch a series of massive blows all along the front in order to roll the entire German army out of the USSR. In other words, the Germans thought too small: they thought of an offensive aimed at a particular sector of the front, while the Soviets in fact envisioned attacking everywhere in a series of rolling punches.

The correlation of forces favored Soviet intentions. Army Group Center, which had borne the brunt of the Moscow offensive, remained a shell of its former self. Drained by losses, transfers of units to other army groups (including almost all of its armor to meet the expected attack in the Ukraine), and a lack of replacements, it was primarily an infantry army little different from its predecessor during the First World War. A total of about 800 000 men manned the front lines, supported by one panzer division and very few aircraft. The paucity of German forces was partly compensated for by a defensive network which had been built during the months it had remained essentially stationary. But backing this partly fortified line were only 550 armored vehicles, of which 480 were not tanks at all but assault guns. The army group also had a total of about 9500 artillery guns and mortars. This was not, even by German standards, a powerful force.

While the German units were a tattered remnant of the large and well-equipped force which had tried to take Moscow two years earlier, the Soviet forces marshaled for the operation were truly formidable. A total of 118 rifle divisions, eight tank corps, six cavalry divisions, and 14 air defense divisions, about 1 700 000 men, composed First Baltic, Third Belorussian, Second Belorussian, and First Belorussian *Fronts*. These included 2715 tanks and 1355 assault guns (a 6–1 advantage over the Germans), over 10 500 artillery guns, 2300 multiple rocket launchers, and over 11 500 mortars. The greatest discrepancy between the two forces was in air power: 5300 Soviet craft compared to just 839 German aircraft.

Finally, the Red Army had the assistance of the enormous partisan units gathered in the rear of Army Group Center. Although accurate numbers are elusive, by June 1944 there were about 270 000 organized partisans behind the Army Group's lines. These units, over 200 of them, were given demolition and reconnaissance missions by the Soviet command, especially against the German communications and rail networks. These actions made significant contributions to the Soviet effort by disrupting, at least temporarily, German communications.

'Operation Bagration:' The Soviet codeword for the massive and overwhelmingly successful offensive against Army Group Center during the summer of 1944.

The offensive against Army Group Center in Belorussia, code-named **'Operation Bagration,'** was part of a broad strategic plan. The first blow would come in early June against Finland in order to drive it from the war and free additional Soviet units for action elsewhere. 'Bagration' was the second blow, to be followed rapidly by blows against Army Group North Ukraine and Army Group North, and thus along the entire front. The key was to hit each area quickly and decisively, forcing the Germans to commit any and all reserves, and then hitting just as hard and decisively elsewhere. The plan was thus a kind of macabre dance with carefully orchestrated Soviet steps designed to keep the Germans off balance and unable to respond effectively anywhere. To prevent the German intelligence agencies from discovering this plan (an unlikely event given its general incompetence), a massive deception program (*maskirovka*) was instituted to convince the Germans that the offensive would indeed be launched against Army Group North Ukraine. To prevent the Germans from figuring out that Army Group Center was the actual target, the Red Army utilized clever camouflage, complete radio silence, the planting of false leads, and careful movement of tanks. An entire false army was even created in the Ukraine to add weight to the effect. FHO fell for the ruse and in mid-June issued a report that said the expected offensive would occur either against Army Group North Ukraine or Army Group Center, or both, but that the main effort would be in the Ukraine. While Hitler and the OKH may have been fooled by Soviet deception measures, units of Army Group Center realized the truth. Ninth Army, for example, had detected an immense buildup opposite its forces, especially in artillery. Even though it completely missed some of the more important Soviet assets, including entire tank armies, it realized that the scale of what it had detected was out of the ordinary.

The invasion of France by the Anglo-American forces on 6 June, however, complicated German preparations for the expected attack. The German counterattack in Normandy, delayed and weak, failed to destroy the bridgehead and by the end of the first week the Allies were securely ashore. This new front meant that the few reserves remaining to the Germans would have to be sent to the western front rather than being hoarded in anticipation of the Soviet summer offensive, and Soviet planners intended to use this to their advantage. The need to defeat the Allied invasion and blunt the expected Soviet attack also meant that forces could no longer be transferred back and forth from France to the east no matter how serious the crisis in either theater. German juggling of resources became much more complicated during June 1944.

The Soviet plan for the summer of 1944 was stunningly similar to German conceptions of penetration and exploitation to the rear using armor, but in fact it represented the culmination of a long tradition of the Soviet conception of 'deep operations.' There were several phases to the operation: the first was the penetration of the front lines northwest and southwest of Vitebsk in order to encircle it; double pincers were also to be thrown around Mogilev and Bobruisk. These pincers were then to drive for a second massive encirclement west of Minsk. The hope was that Ninth Army, Fourth Army, and Third Panzer Army, in essence the entire German army group, would thus disappear into a cauldron. At that point the other *fronts* would begin their operations and drive the Germans out of the USSR.

The Soviet summer offensive of 1944 began on 10 June in the far north: Leningrad and Karelian *Fronts* began operations against the Finns and their German allies. By 21 June Finnish defenses were so disrupted that Finland asked the USSR for an armistice, followed by a truce shortly thereafter. The first part of the summer offensives had driven Finland from the war. The next blow came behind the lines in Belorussia. On 8 June partisan groups were instructed to open operations against the rails and supply dumps behind Army Group Center. There were thousands of individual acts of sabotage against railways and rail cars, telephone and telegraph lines, and supply assets scattered behind the army group. If it is true that the partisans never tied down large numbers of German units, it is also nonetheless true that their contributions to the chaos behind Army Group Center in June were substantial (rail traffic, for example, ceased for an entire day).

On 22 June a 'reconnaissance in force' commenced in order to probe German defenses for the weak spots and ensure that all German forward trenches were occupied for a massive artillery bombardment scheduled for the next morning. These probes were so successful that near Vitebsk the conditions for a massive encirclement of German forces in that area were immediately created. German defenses were so weak that Soviet probes were as successful as full-scale operations.

'Operation Bagration' began on 23 June at 0500 with one of the largest artillery bombardments of the entire war. Each of the thousands of artillery guns was allotted an enormous number of shells in order to crush the German infantry before the Red Army even left its trenches. The Soviets used a double rolling barrage: one group of guns fired on the main defensive lines while a second group hit both the main line and the secondary lines. This ensured that all of the enemy was disorganized by the shelling rather than just those in the front trenches. The Red Army had also abandoned its reliance upon massed infantry attacks in favor of concentrated assault groups supported by artillery and heavy weapons; behind them, and clearing a path for additional infantry, were the vast numbers of tanks.

Busch, Ernst von (1885–1945): Field Marshal who commanded an army in June, 1941 and rose to command Army Group Center from November, 1943 until June, 1944.

Very quickly the Soviets achieved breakthroughs all along the line of the Third Panzer Army around Vitebsk. By late that afternoon **Ernst von Busch**, commander of Army Group Center, reported that his forces needed to be pulled back from that area before they were destroyed. He suggested moving back to the Dvina river, but Hitler forbade the surrender of the city. Against Fourth Army the main goal was the major east–west highway leading from Moscow to Minsk and further west, and the Red Army used special forces and massive amounts of armor to assault Orsha. Against Ninth Army the attacks went slowly during the first day, which reinforced German ideas that this was not the main Soviet summer offensive and convinced them not to commit reserves. By the morning of 24 June the defenses along the line near Vitebsk had been pierced in many places and these forced a withdrawal of the German units to the Dvina; but the Red Army had raced through the holes it had cut and was already there as the Germans arrived. This meant that German units around Vitebsk found themselves in serious danger of being enveloped. As it became clear that the Red Army pincers would meet behind Vitebsk and cut off all of its defenders, permission to pull out of this trap was finally granted with the caveat (from Hitler himself) that the city would not be surrendered (it was declared a 'fortified place') but held by a single division while the rest fled westward. The Red Army, however, began the second phase of operations by driving towards the Dvina and encircling all positions east of the river. An entire German corps was isolated and tried to escape to freedom by breaking into small units, but the surging Soviet forces cut the ragged Germans to pieces wherever they were found. By 27 June the isolated defenders of Vitebsk had been either killed or captured with a loss of 28 000 men and the creation of an enormous hole in the German defenses. Much of the blame for these losses can be attributed to Hitler's insistence upon holding untenable 'fortified places,' but much can also be blamed upon the German failure to realize Soviet goals and respond accordingly.

Meanwhile heavy fighting and stout resistance by the Germans at Orsha forced the Soviet commanders to probe for weak spots in order to outflank and avoid the German strong points. By 25 June a breakthrough was achieved south of Orsha and it now became clear, even to the Germans, that all forces east of the Berezina were at risk of being encircled. But because Hitler had specifically forbidden the loss of Orsha, the local commander had secretly ordered his units to fall back to the west. By 26 June Orsha was surrounded and the remaining defenders surrendered that night. This meant that the northern sector of Army Group Center had dissolved into chaos and the Red Army was already at the Dvina and the Dnepr river crossings before the Germans had begun to withdraw. The German northern sector of the front was thus unhinged with nowhere to withdraw and no reserves. The Red Army then exploited its successes towards the Berezina river at Borisov, the same area where Napoleon Bonaparte had suffered grievous losses many years before.

The main Soviet tank forces then began moving towards Minsk from Orsha, threatening the rear area of the entire Army Group. 5th Panzer Division, brought in fresh and deployed east of Minsk to meet this threat, offered a robust resistance. But this resistance merely caused the Soviet commanders to shift their advance around this defensive perimeter, in effect isolating and making 5th Panzer virtually irrelevant. The Soviet Twenty-ninth

Tank Corps managed to cross the Berezina north of Borisov while others crossed south of the town, and by 30 June the Berezina was no longer a feasible German defensive line as advance Red Army units had already crossed it at numerous points and were far to the west. As Borisov fell there remained no obstacles to the Soviet recapture of Minsk. Along the southeastern perimeter of Army Group Center a similar catastrophe had occurred to Ninth Army. On the eastern approaches the Third Soviet Army had broken through the German defenses near Rogachev by 24 June and very quickly the situation became so acute that Busch committed his last reserves, a weak panzer division, to stem the Soviet tide. At nearly the same time, however, Sixty-fifth Army broke through further south and began driving for Bobruisk, thus threatening the entire German Ninth Army from its rear. Rokossovsky's forces were so successful that the weak panzer division which Busch had hoped would rescue the situation was ordered to stop and redeploy to Bobruisk; the result was that it became entangled in such severe traffic jams that it played almost no role in the fighting. As the Soviets continued to push westward it became apparent that Ninth Army, Fourth Army, and Third Panzer Army either already had been or were in imminent danger of being encircled. By 27 June effective German resistance was so disrupted along Ninth Army's perimeter that Rokossovsky ordered his armor to ignore its defenses and head for Baranovichi, about 80 miles southwest of Minsk (and in pre-war Poland).

Amidst this collapse Hitler once again sought and found scapegoats. Furious about the waste of 20th Panzer Division (the weak unit sent scurrying around) Hitler sacked the commander of Ninth Army on 27 June, and Busch himself on 28 June because he had tried to overrule Hitler's 'fortified places' policy. Model, again playing the role of 'fireman' and already the commander of Army Group North Ukraine, was then made commander of Army Group Center as well.

Model proved unable yet again to alter the course of events. On 27 June the Red Army had begun its assault on Bobruisk, where a solitary division had been forced by Hitler to hole up (similar to the unit trapped at Vitebsk). By 29 June another group of 40 000 Germans was surrounded in and around Bobruisk and even though about 15 000 of them were ultimately saved, Bobruisk fell that same day. A Soviet soldier who assaulted the pocket wrote after the war that the fighting around Bobruisk was simply a slaughter of German soldiers [**Doc. 20, p. 122**]. Ninth Army, which had lost nearly 50 000 men in a week, was now effectively destroyed and ceased to function as a viable fighting unit. Rokossovsky then proceeded to move towards Minsk from the south in order to trap all the German units east of that city.

The situation around Minsk, which had been the location of Army Group Center's headquarters, was chaotic. Since it had originally been over 100 miles behind the front it had only a few thousand defenders, reinforced within a few days by roughly 15 000 stragglers from shattered units further east. No one expected this ragtag force to halt the Soviet juggernaut, and on 2 July even Hitler recognized the obvious and ordered its evacuation. It was, as usual, too late: on 3 July the Red Army broke through the remaining defensive lines and the city was taken. This closed yet another pocket around the survivors of Fourth Army who had congregated just east of Minsk. The recapture of Minsk, whose capture by the Germans in June 1941 had caused Stalin's brief collapse, effectively ended all German resistance east of a line running from Daugavpils–Minsk–Pripet Marshes. For several weeks the Soviets pounded the surrounded units into smaller and smaller pieces, and few Germans escaped the slaughter.

On 28 June *Stavka* issued orders for the further exploitation of 'Operation Bagration's' success. The new goals were Brest-Litovsk and Kaunas in the north, and Bialystok and Grodno in the center. Army Group Center was a wreck, with an enormous gap between it and Army Group North which it had no hope of plugging. The Soviet steam roller continued pressing its advantage against the shattered German units, reaching Vilnius by 7 July. The city was, like previous cities, declared a 'fortified place' and again the German defenders were swallowed; this time about 12 000 men were lost. Vilnius itself, the scene of so much suffering by its Jewish residents, was recaptured on 13 July.

By the time the Soviet *fronts* had reached Grodno on 16 July they had begun to run out of steam and the pace of operations slackened as the goals of 'Bagration' had been achieved and the supply trains could not keep pace with operations. But, although slowing down, the Red Army continued to advance, taking Brest-Litovsk on 28 July. But at just the moment when operations against Army Group Center began to slow (13 July), First Ukrainian and Fourth Ukrainian *Fronts* launched their offensive against Army Group North Ukraine. This offensive, called the Lvov–Sandomierz operation after its major goals, would prove to be nearly as destructive as 'Bagration' had been. Konev, commanding First Ukrainian, had the most powerful *front* on the entire Eastern Front, and his goals included driving to the Vistula river south of Warsaw. By 12 July German intelligence had guessed that something was brewing and began pulling out of the forward lines; Konev detected this move and launched his attack the next day in order to catch as many German soldiers as possible in the first trenches.

In this region the Germans offered a powerful defense; this was, after all, where they had expected the Soviets to attack all summer. The Red Army had a difficult time and was unable to pierce easily the German lines until 16 July, when Konev made a bold gamble by shoving two armies into a narrow gap; these managed to exploit their opportunity and by the next day they were at Lvov. The Soviets had planned this offensive to run in phases, and on 18 July the second phase began with Rokossovsky's First Belorussian *Front* opening an offensive northeast of Lublin; this was a powerful blow and within two days the Soviets had broken through and were racing for the city. Konev, meanwhile, had netted 30 000 German prisoners in a pocket east of Lvov while the Germans abandoned Lvov itself on 26 July. By 1 August not only had Lvov been captured but the Red Army reached the suburbs of Warsaw.

Army Group North Ukraine suffered grievously from this offensive, but it fought a spirited defense which prevented it from suffering the same fate as its northern neighbor, Army Group Center. It nonetheless suffered a decisive defeat which brought the Red Army to the gates of Warsaw and the western portion of pre-war Poland. This defeat encouraged the Polish resistance movement to seize the city, and on 1 August most of the city center was seized by the Poles. Hitler decided to hold the city and sent in the SS against the poorly armed rebels; Warsaw again became a battlefield for Poles and Germans. While the exhausted Red Army stood idly by in nearby suburbs the city was retaken by the Germans, but by then much of it had been destroyed. It has long been debated whether Stalin let the Poles fight alone against the Germans because he did not support the particular movement which led the rebellion (it was virulently anti-communist) or whether the Red Army had indeed reached the end of its supply lines. The rebels had acted at that moment, it seems, precisely to prevent the Red Army from entering Warsaw as a victorious conqueror, but the truth, as usual, seems to be that the Red Army had advanced so far so fast that it was simply incapable of making the effort to cross the Vistula and seize Warsaw in the face of a spirited German defense (Bellamy, 2007).

'Operation Bagration' was one of the most successful Soviet operations of the war. Seventeen German divisions were obliterated, and about 350 000 men were erased from the rolls of the *Wehrmacht* (including about 150 000 prisoners). Almost the entire German armored strength in the east (not a powerful force to begin with) had been lost along with a great deal of irreplaceable heavy equipment. Army Group Center was, in fact, little more than a gaping hole on the Eastern Front where shattered and newly arrived units tried to tie together a viable front line. The Germans lost more men and materiel during this battle than at any other battle on the Eastern Front, dwarfing even the disaster at Stalingrad. Soviet losses were staggering too, though for the first time less than the German losses: about 180 000 casualties. More important from the Soviet perspective, however, was that the Germans had been forced to divert resources from Army Group North and Army Group North Ukraine to rebuild Army Group Center, exactly as *Stavka* had planned.

With the conclusion of 'Bagration' the forces involved were in need of resupply and rest. This sector therefore remained relatively quiet until 12 January 1945, when the attack on Berlin began. In the meantime operations commenced against Army Group North.

THE DESTRUCTION OF ARMY GROUPS NORTH AND SOUTH

The destruction of Army Group Center left Army Group North in an extremely precarious position. While pushing Army Group Center out of Belorussia, the Red Army had advanced to positions near Riga which threatened to cut off the entire northern army group, which was still occupying positions on a line near Narva far to the east. Contact between the two army groups had been lost during 'Bagration' and the commander of Army Group North made plans to pull his armies west of Riga, re-establish contact with his southern neighbor, and save his army. But before any concrete steps could be taken, Leningrad *Front* launched its offensive on 17 September 1944 and immediately broke through the German lines. The next day the army group began to withdraw, with Hitler's approval, to a line east of Riga. But the general Soviet offensives (which had begun on 14 September) were trying to reach Riga as well (Daugavpils was taken on 27 July) in order to encircle and destroy the army group. Army Group North managed, with skillful fighting, to extract itself from total destruction by successfully pulling to the Latvian positions, but Riga remained the weak spot in German defenses. By 22 September the Red Army was only 15 miles south of the city while the bulk of Army Group North was still northeast of the city. On 28 September Hitler, realizing the precarious position this large force was facing, permitted it to withdraw to positions west of Riga, but only if Army Group North then launched an attack to push the Soviets back from Riga.

By the end of September the Soviet offensive had not achieved its major goal of splintering Army Group North into fragments and the Germans had instead managed a skillful retreat under heavy enemy pressure. The Army Group was, in fact, in a better position than it had been in July because it withdrew in time to more easily defensible lines, unlike Army Group Center in June and July. The Soviets, keenly aware of the maxim to strike where an enemy is weak rather than strong, therefore shifted their attacks further south towards Memel on the Baltic, hoping to close an even larger pocket around Army Group North even if it withdrew west of Riga. During the week it took for the Soviets to move into position for the new assault, the front settled into relative quiet as the Germans withdrew to the west of Riga. On

5 October the blow finally fell, and Third Panzer Army, very weak and with no tanks, was shattered by the initial attacks. The Red Army drove for the Baltic coast and reached a small port about 20 miles north of Memel, cutting all of Army Group North off from the rest of the German army. This bridgehead was broadened by the Soviets over the following days as Army Group North was gradually pushed into and confined in a peninsula known as the Courland.

Over the course of several weeks a debate then ensued within the German high command regarding how to bring this large force out of the pocket and back into the main battle lines. The debate included concentrating its strength around the city of Liepaja and then driving southward with all its effort into Prussia to re-establish contact with Army Group Center. There were also discussions about evacuating it by sea, but Hitler rejected all ideas about saving the army group, arguing instead that Army Group North must remain where it was, go on the defensive, and serve, in essence, as a 'fortified place.' And so it did, and there it remained, totally unable to have any influence on the course of fighting on the Eastern Front, until May 1945, when, isolated hundreds of miles from the front lines, it finally surrendered. On 26 January 1945 the army group was renamed Army Group Courland, and thus Army Group North, whose original goal had been to take Leningrad, faded from the war on the Eastern Front and memory.

Until recently it had not been entirely clear why Hitler sentenced an entire army group to oblivion. Surely its relatively powerful units could have been useful in the battle for Germany and Berlin, but the failure to remove them in time deprived the *Wehrmacht* of their help. Various reasons have been put forth, most of them centered on the idea that Hitler refused to evacuate the army because of his stubborn insistence upon holding all ground regardless of the cost. In some cases holding ground, no matter how tactically unsound, might have made sense, but Hitler, many believe, adopted this as a matter of course regardless of circumstances. There is no doubt that Hitler gave such orders and that they often defied both military logic and sheer common sense, but in the case of Army Group Courland another explanation has recently been offered. It seems that the presence of this army group in Courland along the Baltic sea permitted the Germans to continue training U-Boat crews in the training grounds of the eastern Baltic. These crews were to man the new submarines that Hitler and the navy believed would make it impossible for the western Allies to use the Atlantic as a shipment lane for their armies in France. Once these had been choked of supplies the Germans could defeat them and then concentrate on the war in the east. In addition, the eastern Baltic had to be protected from Soviet naval vessels so that shipments of iron ore from Sweden could continue without interference. The German presence in Courland thus allowed the Germans to retain some control over the Baltic, an arena which Hitler believed was important for final German victory (Grier, 2007). However true this may be, and it is debatable (beyond a few prototypes, none of the submarines were ever built), the German effort in the east suffered a grievous blow with the loss of Army Group North and Soviet attentions had not yet turned towards the southern army groups.

On 20 August another of the great blows fell, this time on Army Group South (which had been renamed Army Group North Ukraine and Army Group South Ukraine in recognition that the Soviet offensives had split it into halves). Second and Third Ukrainian *Fronts* launched the Yassy–Kishinev operation, which was designed not only to recover the last portion of the USSR still occupied by the Germans but also to drive Romania, a German ally since the early days of the war, from the conflict. Within just a few days both army groups and the Romanian army had been virtually destroyed. On 23 August Romania's king dismissed the pro-German prime minister and on 26 August declared war on Germany. By 31 August the Red Army was in Bucharest and the conquest of Romania had been virtually completed. On 5 September the USSR declared war on Bulgaria, a German ally which had sent no troops to the Eastern Front and had no German troops within its borders. By 9 September a communist coup had overthrown the pro-German government as Third Ukrainian *Front* approached the capital at Sofia and the new government welcomed the Red Army as liberating heroes. The offensives of the summer and fall of 1944 had deprived Germany of its allies Finland, Romania, and Bulgaria, while the two latter nations even provided about 30 divisions who joined the Red Army in its war against the Germans. From 28 September through 20 October the rest of the Balkans was cleared of German forces as Second and Fourth Ukrainian *Fronts* entered Yugoslavia and, in conjunction with Tito's partisans, captured Belgrade on 19 October.

By this time the Germans realized the danger facing their forces in Greece and the Balkans and had begun evacuating Greece, driving and marching almost non-stop through Yugoslavia to the vicinity of Sarajevo. But the Red Army was more concerned with another German ally, Hungary, and on 6 October opened an operation to conquer the eastern portion of the country. Powerful German counterattacks resulted in heavy losses and the eastern portion of Hungary was not conquered until 28 October. The next day an operation to capture Budapest and the western portion of Hungary was launched by Second and Third Ukrainian, which again met stiff German resistance and it was not until 26 December that the city was surrounded with 188 000 Germans trapped inside. On 5 February Hitler ordered an ill-conceived counteroffensive to save Budapest and the fighting in this area continued until 13 February. When this last major group of Germans in the south had been defeated, the Red Army continued its westward advance, reaching Vienna by 14 April. The war in the south was, in effect, over.

THE BATTLE FOR BERLIN

By the fall of 1944 the balance of forces, never in Germany's favor, had become a serious handicap for the German war effort (see Map 5). On 1 October German strength in the east was about 1 800 000 men and about 1900 aircraft, while the Red Army had about 6.4 million men and over 10 000 aircraft (Bellamy, 2007: 635). German production of fuel was rapidly falling to levels which crippled both mobile and air operations, and access to iron ores and vital raw materials was beginning to falter as mines were overrun by the Red Army and trading partners became increasingly less inclined to continue providing raw materials since it was obvious that Germany would lose the war.

The disparity in resources and the incredible collapse of the Eastern Front since June 1944 led *Stavka* to propose an operation it believed could end the war in about six weeks. Neither Army Group South, or rather its successors, or Army Group Courland posed a threat to Soviet forces. Army Group Center was a wreck composed of weak and shattered armies, and Army Groups A and Vistula (the successors to Army Group North) barely deserved the moniker of army group. Rokossovsky's Second Belorussian *Front* would therefore strike northward towards Danzig to cut off Prussia and its few defenders, while Zhukov's First Belorussian and Konev's First Ukrainian would drive for the Oder river, less than 50 miles from Berlin. During a second phase Zhukov and Konev's forces would push straight from the Oder to Berlin. This plan was too ambitious, however, given the realities of supplies and the fact that the Germans, while clearly on their last legs, were still a formidable enemy. The final operation consisted of four phases rather than two: Vistula–Oder, from 12 January through 3 February; East Prussia, from 13 January through 25 February; East Pomerania from 10 February through 4 April; and Berlin, from 16 April through 8 May. During November and December the Red Army therefore rested and re-equipped for its final push towards Berlin. The supply trains ran constantly, bringing an unprecedented number of mortar and artillery shells for each of the *fronts*, as the plan gave artillery a large role in operations.

On 12 January, eight days earlier than planned to relieve pressure on the western Allies still battling in the Ardennes, the offensive began. The artillery barrage was stupendous: there were over 350 guns for every 2.2 miles of front, which meant the guns were literally wheel to wheel. The realization that the German situation was hopeless, despite their fighting skills, had by now reached even average soldiers [**Doc. 21, p. 123**], and the barrage broke the German line in front of First Ukrainian. Zhukov's *Front* also let loose a shattering barrage, firing 315 000 shells in 25 minutes (Bellamy, 2007: 641). By 15 January the Red Army had torn holes in the lines serious enough for Hitler to transfer two divisions from France despite the appalling losses there. The danger was so acute that Hitler moved his headquarters from Prussia to the bunker in Berlin (which he never left). By 17 January Warsaw was taken, followed quickly by Lodz and Krakow. The Red Army advanced very rapidly, about 300 miles in three weeks. By the beginning of February Soviet attention focused on Breslau, a key Silesian industrial city. Konev advanced on the city in such a way as to permit the Germans to withdraw, as Stalin had made it clear he wanted the industrial assets of Silesia to fall into Soviet hands as intact as possible. But very tough fighting prevented the Soviets an easy victory, and Breslau did not fall until 15 April.

On 27 January Konev's forces reached the Polish town of Osweicim, known to the Germans as Auschwitz. While most prisoners had been evacuated, the Red Army found evidence of the great tragedy which had occurred there, including the clothing and possessions of the hundreds of thousands of people who had been murdered there and in the death camp at Birkenau (which had been partly destroyed by the retreating Germans). During this period the Red Army also liberated Maidanek and Treblinka (which had also been destroyed), and in fact all of the German death camps.

While Konev was taking Silesia, Zhukov drove westward for Posen, which held out for a month (until 23 February), and then Küstrin on the Oder. The latter, as well as the city of Frankfurt-an-der-Oder, were the bridgeheads by which Zhukov hoped to cross the Oder and drive for Berlin. By the end of January, however, both Zhukov and Konev realized that they had run so far that they were beginning to have supply difficulties again. The hold-outs to the rear (such as Posen and Breslau) complicated supply issues and drained resources, as did the lingering presence of German units to the north in Prussia and Pomerania. So during March First Belorussian and First Ukrainian *Fronts* paused to re-equip and rest along the Oder and Neisse rivers while Second Belorussian *Front* conducted operations to clear both Prussia and Pomerania.

With Soviet forces poised to enter Germany proper Hitler panicked; he could not tolerate the idea of Red Army units using resources and assets seized from German sources as they advanced. On 30 March 1945 he therefore issued a decree which ordered the destruction of any and all industrial facilities, power generating facilities, dams, sewer and electrical systems, or any other hallmark of an industrial nation which was about to fall into Soviet hands. This 'Nero decree' thus envisioned the total destruction of Germany as a modern industrial nation in order to stop the Red Army [**Doc. 22, p. 124**].

It was a truly remarkable document which highlights not only Hitler's utter ruthlessness towards the Soviet Union, but even to his own people: how would the Germans, once the war was lost, rebuild their lives?

This pause and the supplies brought to the front created the greatest single armed force ever assembled in wartime: 2 000 000 men, 6250 tanks, 7500 aircraft, 41 600 guns and mortars, and vast amounts of fuel and ammunition. Except for the number of soldiers, the *fronts* directed at Berlin were larger than the German force which had invaded the USSR during 'Barbarossa' and possessed a much greater array of modern weapons, while the German units facing them were shattered wrecks. The two *fronts*, however, were not given explicit directions as to which one would actually take Berlin. The plan, outlined on 1 April, was for Zhukov and Konev to drive west from the Oder and encircle the city while Rokossovsky continued his attacks against the remnants of Army Group Vistula in the north. Stalin had supposedly said that once the two *fronts* had encircled Berlin, 'whoever breaks in first, let him take Berlin' (Bellamy, 2007).

Zhukov had the most difficult task: he held only a tiny bridgehead over the Oder, but into this gap he poured his artillery. He also, in order to blind the Germans as his units attacked in the early morning hours, brought up 140 searchlights to aim at the enemy ground troops. From the Seelow Heights he planned to drive straight through the German defenses and to Berlin; an inelegant approach which promised enormous casualties since the Germans controlled the high ground, but to Zhukov it seemed to be the quickest solution. Konev, on the other hand, preferred a more refined approach: he could cross the Neisse, drive towards Cottbus and then swing around Fourth Panzer Army, trapping its forces in a classic enveloping maneuver.

On 15 April Hitler, realizing that the storm was about to break over Berlin, issued his last directive to the soldiers on the Eastern Front (who were, by this point, fighting well within German borders). Hitler exhorted the men to resist and defend their homes, their families, and threatened that their failure would result in the wholesale destruction of Germany. It was a frightened cry of desperation by a man whose criminal dreams were falling to pieces before his eyes [**Doc. 23, p. 124**].

At 0550 the next morning one of the largest artillery bombardments in the history of warfare began in front of Zhukov's forces; but it fell into largely empty German positions. The German commanders knew the Soviet method of operations and had pulled their troops out of the first line of trenches. Even the searchlights, such a brilliant idea in theory, backfired as the light bounced off the dust and smoke to blind the Red Army rather than the Germans. Zhukov's forces tried to bludgeon their way through Seelow by brute force but the hilly terrain favored the defense and the Germans, who excelled in defensive warfare, offered a tough and tenacious defense. Konev, however, got off to an excellent start and by 17 April he was halfway to Cottbus. As Zhukov tried to batter his way westward, Konev's forces crossed the Spree river (which flows into Berlin) in force with large tank forces and, using the superhighway to Berlin, rode in high speed towards the capital, bypassing and isolating several pockets of German units south of the city.

By 18 April Zhukov's forces had finally broken through the German lines and began spreading across the open plains before Berlin. On 19 April Rokossovsky's forces launched their offensive against Army Group Vistula between Schwedt and Stettin, breaking through quickly and reaching the Elbe river, where it encountered American forces, by 7 May. Konev's drive behind the German lines from Cottbus imperiled German forces south of Berlin and caught Ninth Army and the remnants of Fourth Panzer Army in a pocket about 20 miles south of the city. On 21 April Konev's forces captured the abandoned headquarters of the OKH at Zossen, just south of Berlin. There is a story, probably apocryphal, that a call came in as Red Army soldiers filtered through the building and a private answered with the words 'Ivan here . . .' (Bellamy, 2007). On 24 April elements of Zhukov's and Konev's forces met near Berlin's Schonfeld airport (which is still in operation today), which meant that the two *fronts* had linked up in front of Berlin and destroyed all German opposition east of the city. The next day First Belorussian and First Ukrainian *Fronts* met at Ketzin, west of the city: Berlin was surrounded. More ominously for German forces, soldiers of the US Army and the Red Army met at several places along the Elbe river south of Berlin on 25 April: the Western and Eastern Fronts had merged.

On 26 April the Soviets began penetrating into Berlin itself, especially towards the central sector around the zoo and the government sector. The Soviets used their tanks and artillery to blast directly into buildings at point-blank range at a shattering rate; along the once fashionable street of Unter den Linden, east of the Brandenburg Gate, were 500 guns, again wheel-to-wheel, firing directly into the government district. By 28 April the Red Army was approaching the Reichstag and slowly closing the ring around the last German forces in Berlin. By noon on 30 April the assault on the Reichstag began, and by late afternoon the Red flag was hoisted over the building. At roughly the same time, around 3:00 pm, Hitler committed suicide in his bunker beneath the Chancellery.

Around 4:00 pm on 1 May a messenger told Chuikov, of Stalingrad fame, that Hitler had killed himself. Chuikov replied that 'We know that,' lying in order to impress and confuse his visitor, the chief of the German army staff. The two men then began to negotiate Berlin's surrender, but the German proved so intractable that Chuikov decided to launch a massive bombardment of the city center. On 2 May the commander of German forces in Berlin negotiated with Chuikov and ordered all resistance within the city to cease; at 03:00 on 2 May the fighting ceased and Berlin officially surrendered. The fighting on the Eastern Front was, except for the final surrender of Army Group Center near Prague on 11 May, over.

5

Assessment

An assessment of the war on the Eastern Front has to take into consideration the factors which led to German defeat and Soviet victory: the costs in terms of human lives and physical destruction, and the impact it had upon the post-war world.

The major question about the defeat of Germany must be why it took so long, if Germany had so many disadvantages, for the USSR to defeat it. Closely related to this question is a second one: why was its victory so costly for the Soviets? Part of the answer to these questions lies in the outstanding German victories of the summer of 1941. The incredible losses suffered by the Red Army permitted the Germans to drive deeply into the USSR. The Red Army was not capable of fighting the kind of mobile, modern warfare practiced by the Germans and necessary to drive them out. As the Red Army rebuilt itself after the catastrophic losses it had to learn anew, and quickly, in order to put a brake on further German advances during 1942. As it 'learned to fight' it gradually halted and then began pushing back an exhausted Germany. The remarkable resilience of the Soviet system permitted it to survive the initial onslaught, maintain its cohesion, and then build an effective counterweight to the *Wehrmacht*. None of this had been expected by German planners; they had not foreseen or planned for Soviet resilience but rather for Soviet collapse. Instead of a leaderless mass of Slavic 'sub-humans' the Germans found some of the best commanders and units of any army at any time.

The USSR was also able to defeat the Germans because it belonged to a coalition whose partners' ability to wage war far surpassed those of Germany and its allies. Had the Soviets not been able to replace the stupendous losses of 1941 the war might have turned out differently; as it turned out the USSR and its allies produced far greater quantities of tanks, vehicles, guns, and the preponderance of these weapons slowly began to cancel the slight edge which German troops possessed in skill and tactics. In addition, the Allies were able to coordinate offensives and invasions in such a way as to keep the

Germans off balance and unable to deploy effectively their limited reserves. The invasions of Italy, Sicily, and North Africa may have been small in comparison to battles on the Eastern Front, but they nonetheless deprived the Germans of forces which could have been used in the east. Allied bombing gradually eroded the German ability to fight modern war, especially when oil refining facilities were targeted in 1944. The resulting shortage of fuels and oils had an effect on German mobility on all fronts. The advantage in materiel enjoyed by the Allied coalition created the conditions whereby a continually improving Red Army faced an increasingly feeble enemy.

The disadvantage in materiel which operated against German plans was compounded by a flawed invasion plan. Not only were the tasks extremely ambitious and not adequately planned, but German intentions for the conquered territories and the resulting mass murders committed while trying to enact these plans, ultimately meant that even anti-communists and people who had no desire to see the USSR return became enemies in the German rear areas. The entire German effort in the east, from its inception through its execution, was deeply flawed, and the Red Army was able to use these errors to its advantage.

The human and physical costs of the war in the east were enormous. By May 1945 much of eastern Europe lay in ruins. Millions of people had been killed, wounded, made homeless, and lost everything. The war on the Eastern Front was a colossal struggle in every meaning of the word. The current estimate for the number of deaths in the USSR is 26–27 million, with 8.6 million of these soldiers in the Red Army; this was approximately 14 per cent of the total population. German losses also numbered in the millions, including 5.6 million *Wehrmacht* deaths, the majority of these on the Eastern Front (Bellamy, 2007). This massive demographic loss continues to be reflected in the population statistics of the Russian Federation and Ukraine as the population of these nations ages. Dozens of Soviet cities, thousands of towns and villages, and innumerable factories, farms, and homes were either totally (like Kharkov and Stalingrad) or partly destroyed (like Kiev). An entire generation saw its hopes, dreams, families, futures, and lives wiped out.

The losses in the USSR are even more staggering when compared to the losses suffered by other combatants during the war. The United States suffered approximately 418 000 deaths during the war (in both the European and Pacific theaters), about .3 per cent of the total population, while Britain, which fought since September 3, 1939, suffered the loss of approximately 450 000 people, 385 000 of them military (about 1 per cent of the total mainland population). These are staggering numbers and represent tragedies on an enormous scale. And yet the Red Army lost more than either the United States or Britain during the border battles in June and July 1941, and almost as many during the large-scale individual battles of 1942–44 (nearly a million died fighting for Moscow and Leningrad, for example). The Battle of the Bulge, which looms so large in American military history, saw the deaths of 19 000 American servicemen (about 75 000 total casualties) during a period of about three weeks; these were the largest combat losses suffered by the United States during the Second World War. And yet this was, on average, equivalent to about three days of combat deaths by the Red Army on the Eastern Front. It is estimated, for example, that nearly one million civilians died in Leningrad alone, or more than the total United States and British deaths combined.

The vast disparity between the losses borne by the USSR and those of the western Allies created a feeling among Soviet citizens that it was they who had borne the brunt of defeating Nazism. No other combatant suffered anywhere near the losses suffered by Soviet civilians; less than 2000 American civilians were killed during the war, mostly at Pearl Harbor and the Philippines. No American cities or towns suffered any damage at all during the war, and no American civilians were bundled out of their homes and herded into a barn to be shot or burned to death. Yet more than 20 million Soviet civilians, including millions of Jews, were ruthlessly murdered. The effort to destroy the Nazi threat, from the Soviet viewpoint, was a Soviet victory achieved by the blood of the Soviet people. And yet the western half of Europe was occupied by the United States and Britain as they evicted the *Wehrmacht* from those countries. The victory therefore had to be shared and the unequal burden led to tensions between the victors, especially in the post-war treatment of Germany. Soviet leaders were determined to make the Germans pay for their crimes against the USSR and sentenced even average soldiers to lengthy prison sentences after the war. Many of the POWs captured by the Red Army never returned home because they died in prison in Siberia after being declared war criminals. Soviet policy was equally harsh on the German leadership, insisting that it suffer for unleashing a war of annihilation upon the peoples of the USSR.

The USSR had little interest in rebuilding Germany and de-industrialized broad swaths of eastern Germany as it dismantled thousands of factories, power plants, and economic assets for shipment eastward as reparations for the thousands of facilities destroyed by the Germans. The USSR also had few reasons to be generous with most eastern European nations as these had, in one way or another, allied themselves to Germany during the war. Romania, Hungary, and Albania had even sent troops to the Eastern Front to fight with the Germans. The virulent anti-communism common in these countries before the war also meant that the Soviets were suspicious of any popular movements which could threaten the communist governments established at the end of the war. Force therefore played a large role in maintaining communist control of the eastern bloc.

The physical destruction of the war caused enormous difficulties for Europeans as well. Vast areas of Europe were in ruins due to combat, bombing, and neglect. This destruction was most complete in Germany and eastern Europe, which bore the brunt of both Allied bombing and the conflict between the Soviet Union and Germany. The Second World War shattered and bankrupted European economic and military power, with the singular exception of the USSR, leaving the United States and the USSR as the only world powers by 1945.

As the western half of Europe was rebuilt during the 1950s and 1960s, Soviet planners hesitated to invest scarce capital in these former enemies and eastern Europe therefore suffered economic stagnation which continues to affect these nations today. There was little incentive for the USSR to invest capital in rebuilding the war-torn economies of its occupied territories since the rebuilding of the Soviet Union received first priority for any funds designated for reconstruction. The extreme violence and destruction which resulted from the war therefore created a legacy of neglect by the USSR for the countries it had freed from German occupation.

The Soviets had no desire to see a united (and therefore powerful) Germany arise from the ashes of defeat, and for many years discouraged and persecuted all signs of German nationalism in their zone of control. This extended to nationalism in the communist countries of eastern Europe as well, and any overly nationalist agendas were viewed with extreme suspicion in Moscow. This refusal to grant elementary freedoms conflicted with the attitudes in the west and, over the years, led to tensions which eventually divided the alliance between the USSR and the United States. American perceptions that the USSR was imposing communism on the eastern half of Germany and eastern Europe and Soviet perceptions that the United States was not committed to the total eradication of Nazism gradually dissolved the trust which had grown up between the two nations during the war. The spread of communism across the globe after 1945 only exacerbated these tensions.

In June 1941, when 'Operation Barbarossa' was launched, the only communist nation in the world was the USSR. By 1947 not only had the Soviet Union survived the war but it had liberated several European nations from German control and instituted communist governments in eight of them: Poland, what would become East Germany, Czechoslovakia, Hungary, Romania, Yugoslavia, Bulgaria, and Albania. In addition it regained control of Estonia, Latvia, and Lithuania. It is difficult to imagine how these nations could have become communist without the war, especially given the virulent anti-communism among influential circles in those nations. Within a few years the Chinese also created a communist government and vast areas of the globe fell under the domination of communist governments. Several wars fought during the second half of the twentieth century were fought precisely to prevent the spread of communism across the globe, including Korea and Vietnam, and several nations became cold war battlefields where the USSR and the United States fought out their political differences. The Red Army maintained a presence in the nations of eastern Europe until the very end of the Soviet Union, while the United States still has bases in several European countries (especially in Germany). These occupations spelled the end of a period of world history where the destinies of peoples around the globe were determined in the capitals of Europe, especially in London, Berlin, and Paris. Germany, one of the great world powers before 1918, was in fact divided between the victors of the Second World War and had no say in its own affairs for several years. But even had it been an independent nation capable of intervening in world affairs, the two superpowers of the USSR and the United States set the agenda even for European affairs. The Second World war on the Eastern Front created the conditions by which the USSR came to dominate eastern Europe and world affairs for much of the second half of the twentieth century.

Part 2

DOCUMENTS

Document 1   NAZI-SOVIET PACT, 23 AUGUST 1939

To the shock of much of the world, in August 1939 the leadership of the two rival ideologies made a non-aggression pact; the secret annex divided eastern Europe into spheres of influence.

Article 1   The two contracting parties undertake to refrain from any act of violence, any aggressive action, or any attack against one another, whether individually or jointly with other powers.

Article 2   In case any of the contracting parties should become the object of warlike acts on the part of a third power, the other contracting party will not support that third power in any form.

Article 6   The present Treaty is concluded for a period of ten years with the provision that unless one of the contracting parties denounces it one year before the end of this period the duration of the validity of this treaty is . . . automatically prolonged for another five years.

Secret Additional Protocol:

In the event of a territorial and political transformation of the territories belonging to the Polish State, the spheres of interest of both Germany and the USSR shall be bounded by the line of the rivers Narew, Vistula, and San.

Source: Nazism 1919–1945 Volume 3 Foreign Policy, War and Racial Extermination: A Documentary Reader, edited by J. Noakes and G. Pridham, new edition 2001, ISBN 978 0 85989 602 3 pp. 135–6.

Document 2   HITLER LETTER TO MUSSOLINI, 21 JUNE 1941

Duce!

I am writing this letter to you at a moment when months of anxious deliberation and continuous nerve-wracking waiting are ending in the hardest decision of my life. I believe – after seeing the latest Russian situation map and after appraisal of numerous other reports – that I cannot take the responsibility of waiting longer, and above all, I believe that there is no other way of obviating this danger – unless it be further waiting, which, however, would necessarily lead to disaster in this or the next year at the latest. The situation: England has lost this war. With the right of the drowning person, she grasps at every straw which, in her imagination, might serve as a sheet anchor. Nevertheless, some of her hopes are naturally not without a certain logic. England has always thus far conducted her wars with help from the Continent. The destruction of France – in fact, the elimination of all west-European positions – is directing the glances of the British warmongers continually to the place from which they tried to start the war: to Soviet Russia. As far as the war in the East is concerned, Duce, it will surely be difficult, but

I do not entertain a second's doubt as to its great success. Whatever may now come, Duce, our situation cannot become worse as a result of this step; it can only improve. . . . Should England nevertheless not draw any conclusions from the hard facts that present themselves, then we can, with our rear secured, apply ourselves with increased strength to the dispatching of our opponent. . . .

In conclusion, let me say one more thing, Duce. Since I struggled through to this decision, I again feel spiritually free. The partnership with the Soviet Union, in spite of the complete sincerity of the efforts to bring about a final conciliation, was nevertheless often very irksome to me, for in some way or other it seemed to me to be a break with my whole origin, my concepts, and my former obligations. I am now happy to be relieved of these mental agonies.

With hearty and comradely greetings, Adolf Hitler.

Source: United States Department of State (1948) *Nazi–Soviet Relations 1939–1941: Documents from the Archives of the German Foreign Office* (Washington, DC: USGPO), pp. 349–53.

DIRECTIVE FOR 'OPERATION BARBAROSSA' **Document 3**

This document laid down the guidelines which the Wehrmacht was to follow in planning the invasion of the USSR.

Directive Number 21, Case Barbarossa, December 18, 1940.

The German Armed Forces must be prepared, even before the conclusion of the war against England, *to crush the Soviet Russia in a rapid campaign* ('Case Barbarossa').

The *Army* will have to employ all available formations to this end, with the reservation that occupied territories must be insured against surprise attacks.

The *Air Force* will have to make available for this Eastern campaign supporting forces of such strength that the Army will be able to bring land operations to a speedy conclusion. . . . The main efforts of the *Navy* will continue to be directed against *England* even during the Eastern campaign. . . .

Preparations . . . will be concluded by 15 May 1941. . . .

The preparation of the High Commands will be made on the following basis:

The bulk of the Russian Army stationed in Western Russia will be destroyed by daring operations led by deeply penetrating armored spearheads. Russian forces still capable of giving battle will be prevented from withdrawing into the depths of Russia.

The enemy will be energetically pursued and a line will be reached from which the Russian Air Force can no longer attack German territory. The final objective of the operation is to erect a barrier against Asiatic Russia on the general line Volga–Archangel. . . .

In the theater of operations, which is divided by the Pripet Marshes into a Southern and Northern sector, the main weight of attack will be delivered in the *Northern* area. Two Army Groups will be employed there.

The more southerly of these two Army Groups (in the center of the whole front) will have the task of advancing with powerful armored and motorized formations from the area about and north of Warsaw, and routing the enemy forces in White Russia. This will make it possible for strong mobile forces to advance northward and, in conjunction with the Northern Army Group operating out of East Prussia in the general direction of Leningrad, to destroy enemy forces operating in the Baltic area. Only after the fulfillment of this first essential task, which must include the occupation of Leningrad and Kronstadt, will the attack be continued with the intention of occupying Moscow, an important center of communications and of the armaments industry.

When the battles north and south of the Pripet Marshes are ended the pursuit of the enemy will have the following aims:

In the *South* the early capture of the Donets Basin, important for war industry. In the *North* a quick advance to Moscow. The capture of this city would represent a decisive political and economic success and would also bring about the capture of the most important railway junctions. . . .

Source: H. Trevor-Roper (ed.) (1964) *Blitzkrieg to Defeat: Hitler's War Directives, 1939–1945* (New York: Holt, Rinehart & Winston), pp. 48–52.

Document 4   DIRECTIVE FOR SPECIAL AREAS DURING 'OPERATION BARBAROSSA,' 13 MARCH 1941

This decree gave Heinrich Himmler full authority to carry out 'special tasks' behind the front during the invasion of the USSR. The Einsatzgruppen operated under this order.

In the area of operations, the *Reichsführer SS* is, on behalf of the Führer, entrusted with *special tasks* for the preparation of the *political administration*, tasks which result from the struggle which has to be carried out between two opposing political systems. Within the realm of these tasks, the Reichsführer SS shall act independently and under his own responsibility. . . . Details shall be arranged directly through the OKH with the Reichsführer SS.

Source: Office of the US Chief of Counsel for Prosecution of Axis Criminality (1946) *Nazi Conspiracy and Aggression* (Washington, DC: USGPO), vol. III, p. 447.

DECREE FOR THE CONDUCT OF COURTS-MARTIAL IN THE EAST,   **Document 5**
13 MAY 1941

This decree removed all German soldiers from the possibility of facing a court-martial for any crimes committed during the invasion. This permitted the murder of anyone whom the soldiers decided posed a threat.

I. 2. Guerrillas are to be killed ruthlessly by the troops in battle or during pursuit.

3. Also all other attacks of enemy civilians . . . are to be fought by the troops at the place of the attack with the most extreme measures until annihilation of the attacker.

4. In cases where measures of this kind were neglected or not immediately possible, elements suspected of offense will be brought at once before an officer. He decides whether they are to be shot.

II. 1. For offenses committed by members of the *Wehrmacht* and its employees against enemy civilians, prosecution is not compulsory, not even if the offense is at the same time a military crime or violation.

2. While judging offenses of this kind, it should be considered in every case, that the breakdown in 1918, the time of suffering of the German people after that, and the numerous blood sacrifices of the movement in the battle against national socialism were decidedly due to the Bolshevist influence, and that no German has forgotten this.

Source: Office of the US Chief of Counsel for Prosecution of Axis Criminality (1946) *Nazi Conspiracy and Aggression* (Washington, DC: USGPO), vol. III, pp. 637–8.

'COMMISSAR DECREE,' 6 JUNE 1941   **Document 6**

During the preparation for 'Operation Barbarossa' several decrees regulating behavior on the eastern front were issued by the Germans. Generally known as the 'Criminal Orders,' one of the most notorious decreed how Soviet commissars would be treated when captured.

In the struggle against Bolshevism, we must *not* assume that the enemy's conduct will be based on principles of humanity or of international law. In particular, hate-inspired, cruel, and inhuman treatment of prisoners can be expected on the part of *all ranks of political commissars*, who are the real leaders of resistance.

The attention of all units must be drawn to the following:

1. To show consideration to these elements during this struggle or to act in accordance with international rules of war is wrong and endangers both our own security and the rapid pacification of conquered territory.

2. Political Commissars have initiated barbaric, Asiatic methods of warfare. Consequently, they will be dealt with *immediately* and with maximum severity. As a matter of principle they will be shot at once whether captured *during operations or otherwise showing resistance.*

The following regulations will apply:

2. On capture they [commissars] will be immediately separated from other prisoners on the field of battle. This is essential to prevent them from influencing in any way the other prisoners. Commissars will not be treated as soldiers. The protections afforded by international law to prisoners of war will not apply in their case. After they have been segregated they will be liquidated.

Source: Martin Broszat, Hans-Adolf Jacobson, and Helmut Krausnick (1968) *Anatomy of the SS State*, translated by Richard Barry (New York: Walker & Company), pp. 532–4.

Document 7   STALIN'S SPEECH ON 3 JULY 1941

Comrades! Citizens! Brothers and sisters! Men of our army and navy! I am addressing you, my friends! The perfidious military attack on our motherland, begun on June 22 by Hitler Germany, is continuing. In spite of the heroic resistance of the Red Army, and although the enemy's finest divisions and finest air force units have already been smashed and have met their doom on the field of battle, the enemy continues to push forward, hurling fresh forces into the attack. . . . A grave danger hangs over our country. . . . The enemy is cruel and implacable. He is out to seize our lands . . . , to seize our grain and oil. . . . He is out to restore the rule of landlords, to restore tsarism, to destroy national culture and the national existence of the Russians, Ukrainians, Byelorussians, Lithuanians, Letts, Estonians, Uzbeks, Tatars, Moldavians, Georgians, Armenians, Azerbaidjanians, and the other free peoples of the Soviet Union. . . . Thus the issue is one of life or death for the Soviet State, for the peoples of the USSR, the issue is whether the peoples of the Soviet Union shall remain free or fall into slavery. . . . In areas occupied by the enemy, guerrilla units, mounted and on foot, must be formed, diversionist groups must be organized to combat enemy troops, to foment guerrilla warfare everywhere, to blow up bridges and roads, damage telephone and telegraph lines, set fire to forests, stores, transports. In the occupied regions conditions must be made unbearable for the enemy and all his accomplices. They must be hounded and annihilated at every step, and all their measures frustrated. This war with fascist Germany cannot be considered an ordinary war. It is not only a war between two armies, it is also a great war of the entire Soviet people against the German fascist forces. . . . All our forces for support of our heroic Red Army and our glorious Red Navy! All forces of the people – for the demolition of the enemy! Forward, to our victory!

Source: Joseph Stalin (1945) *The Great Patriotic War of the Soviet Union* (New York: International Publishers), pp. 9–17.

DECREE ON THE TREATMENT OF CIVILIANS, 23 JULY 1941 **Document 8**

This decree permitted the armed forces to treat Soviet citizens with abso-lute terror in order to obtain tranquility behind the lines.

6. In view of the vast size of the occupied areas of the East, the forces avail-able for establishing security in these areas will be sufficient only if all resist-ance is punished not by legal prosecution of the guilty, but by the spreading of such terror by the occupying forces as is alone appropriate to eradicate every inclination to resist amongst the population. . . . The Commanders must find the means of keeping order within the regions where security is their responsibility, not by demanding more security forces, but by applying suitable, draconian measures.

Source: Office of the US Chief of Counsel for Prosecution of Axis Criminality (1946) *Nazi Conspiracy and Aggression* (Washington, DC: USGPO), vol. VI, p. 876.

HALDER'S DIARY, 3 JULY 1941 **Document 9**

This entry from Halder's diary reflects the almost unlimited confidence of the German leadership during the first few months of the war.

On the whole, then, it may be said even now that the objective to shatter the bulk of the Russian army this side of the Dvina and Dnieper has been accom-plished. . . . It is thus probably no overstatement to say that the Russian

Campaign has been won in the space of two weeks. Of course, this does not yet mean that it is closed. The sheer geographical vastness of the country and the stubbornness of the resistance, which is carried on with all means, will claim our efforts for many more weeks to come.

Source: Franz Halder (1988) *The Halder War Diary, 1939–1942*, edited by Charles Burdick and Hans-Adolf Jacobsen (Novato, CA: Presidio Press), pp. 446–7.

Document 10   HALDER'S DIARY, 11 AUGUST 1941

Just a few weeks after his earlier entry Halder admits that the Germans have made several mistakes, foremost the evaluation of the USSR's abilities.

The whole situation makes it increasingly plain that we have underestimated the Russian colossus, who consistently prepares for war with the utter ruthless determination so characteristic of totalitarian states. . . . At the outset of the war, we reckoned with about 200 enemy divisions. Now we have already counted 360. These divisions indeed are not armed and equipped to our standards, and their tactical leadership is often poor. But there they are, and if we smash a dozen of them, the Russians simply put up another dozen. The time factor favors them, as they are near their own resources, while we are moving farther and farther away from ours. And so our troops, sprawled over an immense front line, without any depth, are subjected to the incessant attacks of the enemy. Sometimes these are successful, because too many gaps must be left open in these enormous spaces.

Source: Franz Halder (1988) *The Halder War Diary, 1939–1942*, edited by Charles Burdick and Hans-Adolf Jacobsen (Novato, CA: Presidio Press), p. 506.

Document 11   FIELD MARSHAL WALTER VON REICHENAU'S ORDER, 10 OCTOBER 1941

Reichenau was the commander of 6th Army during the initial advance into the USSR. This order was so well received among the military command that it was distributed by the high command to all army groups in the east. The implication is that the soldiers are not shooting enough enemy combatants.

Subject: Conduct of Troops in Eastern Territories
    [T]he soldier must have full understanding of the necessity of a severe but just revenge on subhuman Jewry. The Army has to aim at another purpose, i.e., the annihilation of revolts in the hinterland which, as experience proves,

have always been caused by Jews. The combating of the enemy behind the front line is still not being taken seriously enough. Treacherous, cruel partisans and unnatural women are still being made prisoners of war and guerrilla fighters dressed partly in uniforms or plain clothes and vagabonds are still being treated as proper soldiers, and sent to prisoner of war camps. . . . The indifference of numerous apparently anti-Soviet elements, which originates from 'wait and see' attitude, must give way to a clear decision for active collaboration. . . . The fear of the German counter-measures must be stronger than the threats of the wandering Bolshevistic remnants. Being far from all political considerations of the future the soldier has to fulfill two tasks:

1. *Complete annihilation of the false Bolshevistic doctrine of the Soviet State and its armed forces.*

2. *The pitiless extermination of foreign treachery and cruelty and thus the protection of the lives of military personnel in Russia.*

This is the only way to fulfill our historic task to liberate the German people once and forever from the Asiatic-Jewish danger.

Source: Office of the US Chief of Counsel for Prosecution of Axis Criminality (1946) *Nazi Conspiracy and Aggression* (Washington, DC: USGPO), vol. VIII, pp. 585–7.

HITLER COMMENTS ON MOTORIZATION, 29 OCTOBER 1941   **Document 12**

Hitler's comment came at a time when German motorized mobility was rapidly disappearing on the Eastern Front.

In a campaign, it's the infantryman who, when all's said, sets the tempo of operations with his legs. That consideration should bid us keep motorization within reasonable limits. Instead of six horses that used to pull an instrument of war, they've taken to using an infinitely more powerful motor-engine, with the sole object of making possible a speed which is, in practice, unusable – that's been proved. In the choice between mobility and power, the decision in peace-time is given too easily in favor of mobility.

Source: Hugh Trevor-Roper (ed.) (1953) *Hitler's Table Talk, 1941–1944: His Private Conversations* (New York: Enigma Books), p. 94.

Document 13 ORDER FOR GERMAN FORCES TO GO ON THE DEFENSIVE,
8 DECEMBER 1941

The failure to capture Moscow in the fall of 1941 was the first strategic defeat the Germans suffered during the war. This order acknowledges that defeat in subtle ways, e.g., by blaming the failure on weather.

The severe winter weather which has come surprisingly early in the East, and the consequent difficulties in bringing up supplies, compel us to abandon immediately all major offensive operations and to go over to the defensive. The way in which these defensive operations are to be carried out will be decided in accordance with the purpose which they are intended to serve, viz:

a. To hold areas which are of great operational or economic importance to the enemy.

b. To enable forces in the East to rest and recuperate as much as possible.

c. Thus to establish conditions for the resumption of large-scale offensive operations in 1942. . . .

Source: H. Trevor-Roper (ed.) (1964) *Blitzkrieg to Defeat: Hitler's War Directives, 1939–1945* (New York: Holt, Rinehart & Winston), pp. 106–10.

Document 14 HITLER COMMENTS ON THE WINTER OF 1941–42, 12 AND
17 JANUARY 1942

The legend that the winter was one of the causes of the German breakdown originated at the highest levels in Germany. Even Hitler, who should have known better, believed the weather caused the collapse.

January 12: The supplying of the front creates enormous problems. In this matter, we've given proof of the most magnificent gifts of improvisation. Amongst the unforseen matters in which we've had to improvise was that catastrophe of the temperature's falling, in two days, from 2 below zero to 38 below. That paralyzed everything, for nobody expected it. . . . Even this year the winter wouldn't have caused us any difficulties if it hadn't surprised us by its suddenness. . . . In such temperatures, we're obliged to have recourse to traction by animals. On the front in Leningrad, with a temperature of 42 below zero, not a rifle, a machine-gun or a field-gun was working, on our side. But we've just received the oil we unfortunately lacked two months ago.

January 17:   The staggering blow for us was that the situation was entirely
unexpected, and the fact that our men were not equipped for
the temperatures they had to face. If the frost hadn't come,
we'd have gone on careering forward – six hundred kilometers,
in some places. We were within a hair's breadth of it. Pro-
vidence intervened and spared us a catastrophe. . . .

Source: Hugh Trevor-Roper (ed.) (1953) *Hitler's Table Talk, 1941–1944: His Private
Conversations* (New York: Enigma Books), pp. 200–201; 220.

Document 15

ORDER FOR 'OPERATION BLUE,' 5 APRIL 1942

*The 'large-scale offensive operations' in the east during 1942 turned out to be
the invasion of the Caucasus, code-named 'Operation Blue.' It was limited in
scope to the area of Army Group South and its goals were primarily economic.*

The winter battle in Russia is nearing its end. Thanks to the unequaled
courage and self-sacrificing devotion of our soldiers on the Eastern front,
German arms have achieved a great defensive success. . . . As soon as the
weather and the state of the terrain allows, we must seize the initiative again,
and through the superiority of German leadership and the German soldier
force our will upon the enemy. Our aim is to wipe out the entire defense
potential remaining to the Soviets, and to cut them off, as far as possible,
from their most important centers of war industry. . . . In pursuit of the original plan for the Eastern campaign, the armies of the Central sector will stand
fast, those in the *North* will capture Leningrad and link up with the Finns,
while those on the *southern flank* will break through into the Caucasus. In
view of the conditions prevailing at the end of winter, the availability of
troops and resources, and transport problems, these aims can be achieved
only one at a time. First, therefore, all available forces will be concentrated
on the *main operations in the Southern sector*, with the aim of destroying the
enemy before the Don, in order to secure the Caucasian oil-fields and the
passes through the Caucasus mountains themselves. . . .

Source: H. Trevor-Roper (ed.) (1964) *Blitzkrieg to Defeat: Hitler's War Directives,
1939–1945* (New York: Holt, Rinehart & Winston), pp. 116–21.

Document 16

SOVIET ORDER CONCERNING DISCIPLINE IN THE RED ARMY, 28 JULY 1942

*During the German advances in the Ukraine the Red Army was relentlessly
pushed back into the interior of the USSR. Part of this may have been strategic*

but Stalin put an end to voluntary withdrawals with this order, number 227. This created penal battalions for those suspected of cowardice as well as blocking detachments to prevent front line units from retreating without orders.

The enemy is throwing new forces forward to the front and, despite increasing losses, is thrusting forwards, bursting into the depths of the Soviet Union, capturing new regions, devastating and smashing our cities and villages, and raping, robbing, and murdering our population. . . . Some foolish people at the front are consoling themselves with discussions that we can retreat farther to the east since we have great territories, much land, and a large population, and that we will always have an abundance of bread. . . . Further retreat means ruin for ourselves and, in addition, ruin for our motherland. Each new shred of territory abandoned by us will strengthen the enemy to the utmost and weaken our defense and our motherland to the utmost. . . . From all this, it follows that it is time to end the retreat. Not a step back! This should now be our main slogan. We must stubbornly defend every position and every meter of Soviet territory to the last drop of our blood and cling to every shred of Soviet land and fight for it to the utmost. . . . The Red Army High Command orders: . . . from one to three (depending on the situation) penal battalions within the fronts, assign all junior and senior commanders . . . who have been guilty of violating discipline by their cowardice, . . . and place them in the most dangerous sectors of the front to give them the opportunity to redeem themselves with their blood for their crimes against the homeland. . . . Form three to five well-armed blocking detachments (of up to 200 men each) within the armies, place them in the immediate rear of unsteady divisions, and, in the event of panic and unauthorized retreat of divisional units, oblige them to shoot the panic-mongers and cowards on the spot. . . .

Source: David M. Glantz (2005) *Companion to Colossus Reborn: Key Documents and Statistics* (Lawrence, KS: University Press of Kansas), pp. 17–21.

Document 17   A GERMAN WITNESS TO A MASS SHOOTING, 5–6 OCTOBER 1942

Hermann Graebe was a German engineer working for the Wehrmacht on the Eastern Front. He made the following affidavit after the war about what some of what he saw. Dubno is in the Ukraine.

On 5 October 1942, when I visited the building office at Dubno, my foreman . . . told me that in the vicinity of the site, Jews from Dubno had been shot in three large pits, each about 30 meters long and 3 meters deep. About 1500 persons had been killed daily. All of the 5000 Jews who had still been living in Dubno before the pogrom were to be liquidated. . . . Thereupon I drove to the site . . . and saw near it great mounds of earth, about 30 meters long and 2 meters high. Several trucks stood in front of the mounds. Armed Ukrainian militia drove the people off the trucks under the supervision of an SS man. . . . [We] went directly to the pits. Nobody bothered us. Now I heard rifle shots in quick succession, from behind one of the earth mounds. The people who had got off the trucks – men, women, and children of all ages – had to undress upon the order of an SS man, who carried a riding or dog whip. . . . Without screaming or weeping these people undressed, stood around in family groups, kissed each other, said farewells, and waited for a sign from another SS man. . . . The latter counted off about 20 persons and instructed them to go behind the earth mound. . . . I walked around the mound and found myself confronted with a tremendous grave. People were closely wedged together and lying on top of each other so that only their heads were visible. . . . I looked for the man who did the shooting. He was an SS man, who sat at the edge of narrow end of the pit, his feet dangling into the pit. The people, completely naked, went down some steps which were cut in the clay wall of the pit and clambered over the heads of the people lying there, to the place to which the SS man directed them. They lay down in front of the dead or injured people. . . . Then I heard a series of shots. I looked into the pit and saw that the bodies were twitching or the heads lying already motionless on top of the bodies that lay before them. . . . The next batch was approaching already. They went down into the pit, lined themselves up against the previous victims, and were shot. . . .

Source: Office of the US Chief of Counsel for Prosecution of Axis Criminality (1946) *Nazi Conspiracy and Aggression* (Washington, DC: USGPO), vol. V, pp. 696–8.

A GERMAN SOLDIER DESCRIBES THE RETREAT IN THE UKRAINE,   **Document 18**
SUMMER 1943

Our mobility, which had always given us an advantage over the vast but slow Soviet formations, was now only a memory, and the disproportion of numbers made even flight a doubtful prospect. . . . The retreat was costly, and reached its climax on the east bank of the river, in an incredible crush of men and materiel, spread out over acres of flat sand, so that each Russian missile was assured a maximum destructive effect. . . . Everyone reached the river, the outer boundary of safety, in a state of indescribable panic, only to find it was necessary to trample on men already there, even drown them, to have any hope of getting onto the wretchedly inadequate vessels, which often foundered before they reached the other side. . . . The west bank meant security and safety, a barrier between us and the Russians. We had dreamed of this safety for so long and so intensely, that we almost felt as if there were a barrier between us and the war itself. . . . Our exhausted brains clung to this fantasy: the west bank was almost the motherland.

Source: Guy Sajer (1967) *The Forgotten Soldier* (Washington, DC: Brassey's), pp. 253–69.

Document 19   'FORTIFIED AREAS' ORDER, 8 MARCH 1944

By this date Hitler was desperate to stop the Red Army from flooding into eastern Europe. He decided to create 'fortified areas' which would serve as linchpins for counter-attacks. This idea failed to turn the tide in Germany's favor.

In view of various incidents, I issue the following orders:

1. A distinction will be made between 'fortified areas,' each under a 'Fortified Area Commandant,' and 'Local strong-points,' each under a 'Battle Commandant.' The 'fortified areas' will fulfil the function of fortresses in former historical times. They will ensure that the enemy does not occupy these areas of decisive operational importance. They will allow themselves to be surrounded, thereby holding down the largest possible number of enemy forces, and establishing conditions favorable for successful counter-attacks. By being included in the main line of battle [strong points] will act as a reserve of defense and, should the enemy break through, as hinges and corner-stones for the front, forming positions from which counter-attacks can be launched. . . .

Source: H. Trevor-Roper (ed.) (1964) *Blitzkrieg to Defeat: Hitler's War Directives, 1939–1945* (New York: Holt, Rinehart & Winston), pp. 159–61.

Document 20   A SOVIET SOLDIER REPORTS ON COMBAT DURING 'OPERATION BAGRATION,' 29 JUNE 1944

Litvin's unit was ordered to cut off possible escape routes for German units surrounded near Bobruisk. A column of about 10 000 Germans suddenly appeared in front of his unit apparently trying to break out of the encirclement.

We opened fire on the Germans, not permitting them to turn in our direction. The Germans were packed so tightly together, and in such a mass, that it was simply impossible to miss. When our command found out that a German column was attempting to break out here, they rushed an anti-tank battery to our support. . . . The fighting was desperate and continued until nightfall. Having lost perhaps half their force, most Germans fell back to the village. Perhaps 1500 Germans managed to break through our lines and escape. On the field of battle remained piles of German corpses and the seriously wounded. In the morning, we woke up and looked out upon the field of carnage. It was quiet. There was no shooting. The rye field was a mousy color from all the fallen Germans in their field gray uniforms. Their corpses lay piled upon one another. . . . By 11:00 am, a stench began rising into the air.

Source: Nikolai Litvin (2007) *800 Days on the Eastern Front*, translated and edited by Stuart Britton, (Lawrence, KS: University Press of Kansas), p. 69.

A GERMAN SOLDIER REPORTS ON FIGHTING ON THE EASTERN FRONT,   **Document 21**
14 JANUARY 1945

This battle took place on the Vistula Front before the Red Army had broken through to invade Prussia. It reflects how far the Wehrmacht had fallen from its glory days, but also the Red Army's tactics.

After exactly two hours the bombardment suddenly broke off. A paralyzing calm fell over the front. It meant that the Russians were moving their fire forward, in order not to endanger their attacking infantry. . . . I thought I could not believe my eyes when on the right I saw that the second company had already retreated a long way. I then saw the enemy rapidly advancing in battalion strength on to the second trench. The Russians went round my company and cut us off. But from the left, charging at the company command post, there came the left wing of a confused brown wave [Red Army soldiers], approaching unstoppably with cries of *Urrah*. But the most shattering thing about the picture was the fact that individual German soldiers were running away in front of assaulting Red Army troops. They were wobbling with exhaustion, without weapons and equipment, plainly at the end of their strength. . . . The miracle happened. The targeted fire from my rifle, and those of the runners, brought the attack to a standstill. The Red Army troops went to ground. Then, pursued by our bullets, they drew back far to the rear and sought to connect up again to the forces on their right. . . . There was no more immediate danger just then. . . . However, the long-term situation seemed hopeless. Sooner or later we would certainly fall into enemy hands.

Source: Armin Scheiderbauer (2003) *Adventures in My Youth: A German Soldier on the Eastern Front, 1941–45* (New York: Helion & Company), pp. 133–4.

Document 22   DECREE FOR THE DESTRUCTION OF GERMAN INDUSTRY, 30 MARCH 1945

Hitler ordered the retreating German army to destroy all facilities which might prove useful to the invading Red Army as well as the Western Allies. This order clarified what was to be destroyed and when it was to be destroyed.

In order to assure uniform implementation of my decree of March 19, 1945, I hereby make the following order:

1. The order already given for destruction of industrial installations is aimed exclusively at preventing the enemy from using these installations and facilities to add to his fighting strength.

2. No measures should be taken which would decrease our own fighting strength. Production must be carried on to the last possible moment, even at the risk of the factory falling into the hands of the enemy before it could be destroyed.

All kinds of industrial installations, including plants for producing food, should not be destroyed unless they are threatened immediately by the enemy.

3. Bridges and other installations for transport must be destroyed in order to deny the enemy their use for a long time, but the same effect can be won with industrial installations by smashing them permanently. . . .

Source: Louis L. Snyder (1981) *Hitler's Third Reich: A Documentary History* (New York: Nelson-Hall), pp. 501–2.

Document 23   HITLER'S LAST PROCLAMATION TO THE EASTERN FRONT, 15 APRIL 1945

By this point the Red Army was only a few dozen miles from Berlin and there were no resources available to the Germans to stop the impending assault upon the capital. Hitler therefore resorted to terrorizing his soldiers into fanatical resistance with images of murder, rape, and the wholesale destruction of Germany. This was Hitler's last general statement to the troops in the east and is replete with fantasy, fabrications, and deceit on his part.

Soldiers of the German Eastern front!

For the last time our deadly enemies the Jewish Bolsheviks have launched their massive forces to the attack. Their aim is to reduce Germany to ruins and to exterminate our people. Many of you soldiers in the East already know the fate which threatens, above all, German women, girls, and children. While the old men and children will be murdered, the women and girls will be reduced to barrack-room whores. The remainder will be marched off to

Siberia. We have foreseen this thrust, and since last January have done everything possible to construct a strong front. The enemy will be greeted by massive artillery fire. Gaps in our infantry have been made good by countless
new units. . . . This time the Bolshevik will meet the ancient fate of Asia – he
must and shall bleed to death before the capital of the German Reich.
Whoever fails in his duty at this moment behaves as a traitor to our people.
. . . Anyone ordering you to retreat will, unless you know him well personally, be immediately arrested and, if necessary, killed on the spot, no matter
what rank he may hold. If every soldier on the Eastern front does his duty in
the days and weeks which lie ahead, the last assault of Asia will crumple, just
as the invasion by our enemies in the West will finally fail, in spite of everything. Berlin will remain German, Vienna will be German again, and Europe
will never be Russian. Form yourselves into a sworn brotherhood, to defend,
not the empty conception of a Fatherland, but your homes, your wives, your
children, and, with them, our future. In these hours, the whole German people looks to you, my fighters in the East, and only hopes that, thanks to your
resolution and fanaticism, thanks to your weapons, and under your leadership, the Bolshevik assault will be choked in a bath of blood. At this moment,
when Fate has removed from the earth the greatest war criminal of all time
[Franklin Roosevelt], the turning-point of this war will be decided.

Source: H. Trevor-Roper (ed.) (1964) *Blitzkrieg to Defeat: Hitler's War Directives,
1939–1945* (New York: Holt, Rinehart & Winston), pp. 212–13.

Further Reading

The Seminar Studies in History series has published several volumes related to the Second World War. In particular see R.J. Overy, *The Origins of the Second World War*, 2nd ed (1998); David Engel, *The Holocaust: The Third Reich and the Jews* (2000); and S.P. MacKenzie, *The Second World War in Europe* (1999). Other titles of interest include D.G. Williamson, *The Third Reich*, 2nd ed (2002); Frank McDonough, *Hitler and the Rise of the Nazi Party* (2003); and Martin Blinkhorn, *Fascism and the Right in Europe, 1919–1945* (2000).

The literature on the war is enormous and much of it is in either German or Russian. This bibliography will concentrate on those titles available in English, with a few of the most essential which are not in English. An invaluable guide to the literature is Rolf-Dieter Müller and Gerd R. Ueberschär, *Hitler's War in the East, 1941–1945: A Critical Assessment* (New York: Berghahn Books, 2002), 2nd ed. The outstanding guide to the war as a whole is the multi-volume set produced by the Research Institute for Military History, Horst Boog, *et al.* (various dates), translated into English as *Germany and the Second World War* (Oxford: Clarendon Press), especially volumes IV and VI, which contain parts relevant to the war in the east.

Hitler's pronouncements about 'living space' and an eastern policy can be found in his published writings, especially Ralph Mannheim's translation of *Mein Kampf* (1943), Chapters XI and XIV, as well as Gerhard Weinberg's recent edition of *Hitler's Second Book* (New York: Enigma Books, 2003), especially Chapters II, IV, VI, XI, XIII, and XVI. They can also be found in the collection of his speeches by Max Domarus, *Hitler: Speeches and Proclamations, 1932–1945* (Wauconda, IL: Bolchazy-Carducci Publishers, originally published 1962), especially volume IV. His casual conversation was also spiced with reflections on his views about the east, and these have been published by Hugh Trevor-Roper as *Hitler's Table Talk, 1941–1944* (New York: Enigma Books, originally published 1953).

The best and most up to date biography of Hitler is Ian Kershaw, *Hitler, 1889–1936: Hubris* (New York: Longman, 1998); and *Hitler, 1936–1945:*

Nemesis (New York: Norton, 2000). For Stalin see Robert Service, **Stalin: A Biography** (Cambridge, MA: Harvard University Press, 2005). For chapter length biographies of the leading Soviet generals see Harold Shukman (ed.), **Stalin's Generals** (New York: Grove Press, 1993); for the German leadership see Correlli Barnett's **Hitler's Generals** (New York: Grove Press, 2003). Most of the German generals who survived the war wrote their autobiographies; these are of uneven quality and because they were interested in promoting a view of the army as a victim of Hitler must be read with great care. See Franz Halder, **The Halder War Diary, 1939–1942** (Novato, CA: Presidio Press, 1988); Fedor von Bock, **The War Diary, 1939–1945** (Atglen, PA: Schiffer Military History, 1996). Memoirs from Germans include Wilhelm Keitel, **The Memoirs of Field Marshall Wilhelm Keitel**, edited by Walter Gorlitz (New York: Cooper Square Press, 1966); Erich von Manstein, **Lost Victories** (Novato, CA: Presidio Press, originally published 1958); Heinz Guderian, **Panzer Leader** (New York: Da Capo Press, originally published 1952). There are also memoirs from the lower ranks, including the widely available and popular Guy Sajer, **The Forgotten Soldier** (Washington, DC: Brassey's, originally published 1957); and more recently Günther K. Koschorrek, **Blood Red Snow: The Memoirs of a German Soldier on the Eastern Front** (Mechanicsburg, PA: Stackpole Books, 2002). The Italian journalist Curzio Malaparte accompanied the initial German invasion forces in June 1941 and published his memoirs about that time as **The Volga Rises in Europe** (Edinburgh: Birlinn, 1951). Older Soviet memoirs, which are problematical due to the nature of Soviet censorship, include Georgii Zhukov, **Marshall Zhukov's Greatest Battles** (New York: Harper & Row Publishers, 1969); as well as **The Memoirs of Marshall Zhukov** (New York: Delacorte Press, 1971), of which there are several versions, each succeeding volume more inclusive than the previous. A very good recent view from the Soviet rank and file is Nikolai Litvin, **800 Days on the Eastern Front** (Lawrence, KS: University Press of Kansas, 2007).

The Holocaust has a literature just as vast as that of the war. One of the most recent books to clearly link the German armed forces and the Holocaust is Wolfram Wette, **The Wehrmacht: History, Myth, Reality** (Cambridge, MS: Harvard University Press, 2006). Also see Donald M. McKale, **Hitler's Shadow War: The Holocaust and World War II** (New York: Cooper Square Press, 2002). To see the connections between partisan fighting and mass murder start with Ben Shepherd, **War in the Wild East: The German Army and Soviet Partisans** (Cambridge, MA: Harvard University Press, 2004). The best recent works on the Eastern Front emphasize its connections to the Holocaust. Representative of this approach are Geoffrey P. Megargee, **War of Annihilation: Combat and Genocide on the Eastern Front, 1941** (London: Rowman & Littlefield Publishers, Inc., 2006); Hannes Heer and Klaus Naumann, **War of Extermination: The German Military in World War II, 1941–1944** (New York: Berghahn Books, 2000).

The best recent analysis of how the German military high command functioned is Geoffrey P. Megargee, **Inside Hitler's High Command** (Lawrence, KS: University Press of Kansas, 2000). The insider's view is best seen in Walter Warlimont, **Inside Hitler's Headquarters, 1939–45** (Novato, CA: Presidio Press, 1964). A collection of the few surviving minutes from the military conferences has been published in Helmut Heiber and David M. Glantz, **Hitler and his Generals: Military Conferences 1942–1945** (New York: Enigma Books, 2003). The discussion regarding the failure of Soviet intelligence to anticipate the German attack is contained within a large literature. See David E. Murphy, **What Stalin Knew: The Enigma of Barbarossa** (New Haven, CT: Yale University Press, 2005). See also Anthony Read and David Fisher, **The Deadly Embrace: Hitler, Stalin, and the Nazi–Soviet Pact, 1939–1941** (New York: Norton, 1988); and James Barros and Richard Gregor, **Double Deception: Stalin, Hitler, and the Invasion of Russia** (Dekalb, IL: Northern Illinois University Press, 1995); and Geoffrey K. Roberts, **The Soviet Union and the Origins of the Second World War, Russo-German Relations and the Road to War, 1933–1941** (Houndmills: Macmillan, 1995).

An extensive discussion of the planning for 'Barbarossa' can be found in Bryan I. Fugate, **Operation Barbarossa: Strategy and Tactics on the Eastern Front, 1941** (Novato, CA: Presidio Press, 1984), as well as Robert Cecil, **Hitler's Decision to Invade Russia, 1941** (New York: David McKay, 1975). The flaws in overall strategic planning can be traced in Heinz Magenheimer, **Hitler's War: Germany's Key Strategic Decisions, 1940–1945** (London: Cassell & Company, 2002). Percy Schramm's critique of Hitler is a good place to start this topic: **Hitler: The Man and Military Leader** (Chicago, IL: Quadrangle Books, 1971). Studies of the war from a larger perspective illuminate many facets which local studies cannot. See, for example, Oscar Pinkus, **The War Aims and Strategies of Adolf Hitler** (New York: McFarland and Company, 2005). For a global perspective on the entire war on all fronts and theaters see Gerhard L. Weinberg, **A World at Arms: A Global History of World War II** (Cambridge: Cambridge University Press, 1994). For overviews of the campaign in the east a good start is David M. Glantz and Jonathan House, **When Titans Clashed: How the Red Army Stopped Hitler** (Lawrence, KS: University Press of Kansas, 1995). John Erickson's classic two volume history, although more than 30 years old, retains much of value: **The Road to Stalingrad: Stalin's War with Germany** (New York: Harper and Row, 1975); and **The Road to Berlin: Stalin's War with Germany** (London: Weidenfeld and Nicolson, 1983). Shorter but still very valuable are Albert Seaton, **The Russo-German War, 1941–1945** (Novato, CA: Presidio Press, originally published 1971); and Alan Clark, **Barbarossa: The Russian-German Conflict, 1941–1945** (New York: Quill, 1965). Among the best must be placed the recent book by Chris Bellamy, **Absolute War: Soviet Russia in the Second World War** (New York: Alfred A. Knopf, 2007).

There are numerous studies of the individual battles and campaigns fought during the war. Albert Seaton's **The Battle for Moscow** (Edison, NJ: Castle Books, 2001), remains useful, as is Rodric Braithwaite, **Moscow, 1941: A City and its People at War** (New York: Alfred A. Knopf, 2006). Andrew Nagorski, **The Greatest Battle: Stalin, Hitler, and the Desperate Struggle for Moscow that Changed the Course of World War II** (New York: Simon & Schuster, 2007) is a good popular history of the battle. The early campaigns by Army Group Center have been reinterpreted by Bryan Fugate and Lev Dvoretsky, **Thunder on the Dnepr: Zhukov-Stalin and the Defeat of Hitler's Blitzkrieg** (Novato, CA: Presidio Press, 2001). Stalingrad is the topic of a vast literature. A decent overview is Edwin P. Hoyt, **The Battle for Stalingrad: 199 Days** (New York: Tom Doherty Associates, 1993). All of David M. Glantz's books on the Eastern Front are worth reading, but for an example of how even Zhukov could fail see **Zhukov's Greatest Defeat: The Red Army's Epic Disaster in Operation Mars, 1942** (Lawrence, KS: University Press of Kansas, 1999). For the final phases of the war see Christopher Duffy, **Red Storm on the Reich: The Soviet March on Germany, 1945** (New York: Da Capo Press, 1993). For the assault on Berlin see Anthony Beevor, **The Fall of Berlin 1945** (New York: Viking Press, 2002); Anthony Read and David Fisher, **The Fall of Berlin** (New York: Norton, 1992). Studies of the Red Army during the war were (and remain) difficult to write. A good recent attempt is Catherine Merridale, **Ivan's War: Life and Death in the Red Army, 1939–1945** (New York: Metropolitan Books, 2006). Another good overview is Roger R. Reese, **Stalin's Reluctant Soldiers: A Social History of the Red Army, 1925–1941** (Lawrence, KS: University Press of Kansas, 1996).

There are numerous documentaries, many of outstanding value. One of the best fairly recent films is by the BBC, *War of the Century: When Hitler fought Stalin* (1999). There is also the excellent German film whose English title is *Downfall* (2004), which details the last ten days of April, 1945 (although not a documentary, it is fairly accurate historically).

There are also numerous board games which permit players to reconstruct the battles on the Eastern Front. *Strategy & Tactics* published a game covering 'Operation Typhoon' in 2006 and occasionally publishes other battles as well (it has published numerous ones in the past). *Against the Odds* published a game on the Soviet assault on Berlin in 2004 ('Fortress Berlin'). There is a game for just about every battle, large or small, on the Eastern Front, and while most of them are long out of print, they can be obtained second-hand (including a very large set of games on the battle of Stalingrad). These are not only enjoyable but enable a deeper understanding of the problems faced by both sides.

References

Barros, James and Richard Gregor (1995) *Double Deception: Stalin, Hitler, and the Invasion of Russia*. Dekalb, IL: Northern Illinois University Press.

Bartov, Omer (1992) *Hitler's Army: Soldiers, Nazis, and War in the Third Reich*. New York: Oxford University Press.

Bellamy, Chris (2007) *Absolute War: Soviet Russia in the Second World War: A Modern History*. New York: Macmillan.

Beevor, Anthony (1998) *Stalingrad*. New York: Viking Publishing.

Birn, Ruth Bettina (1997) 'Two Kinds of Reality? Case Studies on Anti-Partisan Warfare during the Eastern Campaign,' in Bernd Wegner, *From Peace to War: Germany, Soviet Russia, and the World, 1939–1941*. Oxford: Berghahn Books, pp. 277–91.

Boll, Bernd and Hans Safrian (2000) 'On the Way to Stalingrad: The 6th Army in 1941–1942,' in Hannes Heer and Klaus Naumann, *War of Extermination: The German Military in World War II, 1941–1944*. New York: Berghahn Books, pp. 237–71.

Bonwetsch, Bernd (1997) 'The Purge of the Military and the Red Army's Operational Capability during the "Great Patriotic War," ' in Bernd Wegner, *From Peace to War: Germany, Soviet Russia, and the World, 1939–1941*. Oxford: Berghahn Books, pp. 395–414.

Carley, Michael Jabara (1999) *1939: The Alliance that Never Was and the Coming of World War II*. Chicago, IL: Ivan R. Dee.

Citino, Robert M. (2007) *Death of the Wehrmacht: The German Campaigns of 1942*. Lawrence, KS: University Press of Kansas.

Creveld, Martin van (2004) *Supplying War: Logistics from Wallenstein to Patton*. Cambridge: Cambridge University Press.

Duffy, Peter (2003) *The Bielski Brothers: The True Story of Three Men who Defied the Nazis, saved 1,200 Jews, and built a village in the Forest*. New York: HarperCollins.

Fleischhauer, Ingeborg (1997) 'Soviet Foreign Policy and the Origins of the Hitler-Stalin Pact,' in Bernd Wegner, *From Peace to War: Germany, Soviet Russia, and the World, 1939–1941*. Oxford: Berghahn Books, pp. 27–45.

Förster, Jürgen (1997) 'Hitler Turns East-German War Policy in 1940 and 1941,' in Bernd Wegner, *From Peace to War: Germany, Soviet Russia, and the World, 1939–1941*. Oxford: Berghahn Books, pp. 115–33.

Glantz, David M. (1991) *From the Don to the Dnepr: Soviet Offensive Operations, December 1941–August 1943*. London: Frank Cass.

——, (1998) *Kharkov 1942: Anatomy of a Military Disaster*. Rockville Center, NY: Sarpedon.

——, (1999) *Zhukov's Greatest Defeat: The Red Army's Epic Disaster in Operation Mars, 1942*. Lawrence, KS: University Press of Kansas.

——, and Jonathan House (1995) *When Titans Clashed: How the Red Army Stopped Hitler*. Lawrence, KS: University Press of Kansas.

——, and Jonathan M. House (1999) *The Battle of Kursk*. Lawrence, KS: University Press of Kansas.

Grier, Howard D. (2007) *Hitler/Dönitz, and the Baltic Sea: The Third Reich's Last Hope, 1944–1945*. Annapolis, MD: Naval Institute Press.

Gorodetsky, Gregor (1999) *Grand Delusion: Stalin and the German Invasion of Russia*. New Haven, CT: Yale University Press.

Halder, Franz (1988) *The Halder War Diary, 1939–1942*. Novato, CA: Presidio Press.

Hayward, Joel S.A. (1998) *Stopped at Stalingrad: The Luftwaffe and Hitler's Defeat in the East, 1942–1943*. Lawrence, KS: University Press of Kansas.

Headland, Ronald (1992) *Messages of Murder: A Study of the Reports of the Einsatzgruppen of the Security Police and the Security Service, 1941–1943*. Rutherford, NJ: Fairleigh Dickinson University Press.

Heer, Hannes (2000) 'Killing Fields: The Wehrmacht and the Holocaust in Belorussia, 1941–1942,' in Hannes Heer and Klaus Naumann, *War of Extermination: The German Military in World War II, 1941–1944*. New York: Berghahn Books, pp. 55–79.

(2) ——, (2000) 'The Logic of the War of Extermination,' in Hannes Heer and Klaus Naumann, *War of Extermination: The German Military in World War II, 1941–1944*. New York: Berghahn Books, pp. 92–126.

Hill, Alexander (2007) 'British Lend-Lease Aid and the Soviet War Effort, June 1941–June 1942,' *Journal of Military History*, 71:3, July: pp. 773–808.

Hitler, Adolf (1943) *Mein Kampf*. New York: Houghton Mifflin.

——, (2003) *Hitler's Second Book*, edited by Gerhard Weinberg. New York: Enigma Books.

Jäckel, Eberhard. (1981) *Hitler's World-View: A Blueprint for Power*, translated by Herbert Arnold. Cambridge, MS: Harvard University Press.

Jukes, Geoffrey (1970) *The Defense of Moscow*. New York: Ballantine Books.

Liddell Hart, B. H. (1956) *The Red Army: The Red Army 1918–1945, The Soviet Army 1946 to the Present*. New York: Harcourt, Brace and Company.

Longerich, Peter (1997) 'From Mass Murder to the Final Solution: The Shooting of Jewish Civilians during the first months of the Eastern Campaign within the Context of Nazi Jewish Genocide,' in Bernd Wegner, *From Peace to War: Germany, Soviet Russia, and the World, 1939–1941*. Oxford: Berghahn Books, pp. 253–76.

Lower, Wendy (2005) 'The Holocaust and Colonialism in Ukraine: A Case Study of the *Generalbezirk* Zhytomyr, Ukraine, 1941–1944,' Symposium presentation at the Center for Advanced Holocaust Studies, United States Holocaust Memorial Museum, pp. 1–20.

Mawdsley, Evan (2005) *Thunder in the East: The Nazi–Soviet War, 1941–1945*. London: Hodder Arnold.

Megargee, Geoffrey P. (2006) *War of Annihilation: Combat and Genocide on the Eastern Front, 1941*. Lanham, MD: Rowman & Littlefield Publishers, Inc.

Murphy, David E. (2005) *What Stalin Knew: The Enigma of Barbarossa*. New Haven, CT: Yale University Press.

Newton, Steven H. (2006) *Hitler's Commander: Walter Model – Hitler's Favorite General*. Cambridge, MA: Da Capo Press.

Pleshakov, Konstantin (2005) *Stalin's Folly: The Tragic First Ten Days of World War II on the Eastern Front*. Boston, MA: Houghton Mifflin.

Reese, Roger R. (1996) *Stalin's Reluctant Soldiers: A Social History of the Red Army, 1925–1941*. Lawrence, KS: University Press of Kansas.

Robertson, Esmonde M. (1989) 'Hitler Turns from the West to Russia May–December 1940,' in Robert Boyce and Esmonde M. Robertson, *Paths to New Essays on the Origins of the Second World War*. New York: St. Martin's Press, pp. 367–82.

Schüler, Klaus (1997) 'The Eastern Campaign as a Transportation and Supply Problem,' in Bernd Wegner, *From Peace to War: Germany, Soviet Russia, and the World, 1939–1941*. Oxford: Berghahn Books, pp. 205–22.

Shepherd, Ben (2004) *War in the Wild East: The German Army and Soviet Partisans*. Cambridge, MA: Harvard University Press.

Streit, Christian (2004) 'Soviet Prisoners of War in the Hands of the Wehrmacht,' in Hannes Heer and Klaus Naumann, *War of Extermination: The German Military in World War II, 1941–1944*. New York: Berghahn Books, pp. 80–91.

Suvorov, Viktor (1990) *Ice Breaker: Who Started the Second World War?*, translated by Thomas B. Beattie. London: Hamish Hamilton.

Wegner, Bernd (1997) 'Facing the Global War: Germany's Strategic Dilemma after the Failure of "*Blitzkrieg*",' in Bernd Wegner, *From Peace to War: Germany, Soviet Russia, and the World, 1939–1941*. Oxford: Berghahn Books, pp. 611–27.

Wegner, Bernd (2001) 'The War against the Soviet Union, 1942–1943,' in Horst Boog, Werner Rahn, Reinhard Stumpf and Bernd Wegner (eds.) *Germany and the Second World War*. Oxford: Oxford University Press, vol. 6, pp. 841–1215.

Westermann, Edward B. (2005) *Hitler's Police Battalions: Enforcing Racial War in the East*. Lawrence, KS: University Press of Kansas.

Wette, Wolfram (1968) *The Battle for Berlin: End of the Third Reich*. New York: Ballantine Books.

——, (2006) *The Wehrmacht: History, Myth, Reality*. Cambridge, MA: Harvard University Press.

Ziemke, Earl F. (1975) 'Franz Halder at Orsha: The German General Staff Seeks a Consensus,' *Military Affairs*, XXXIX: 4, December: pp. 173–6.

Index

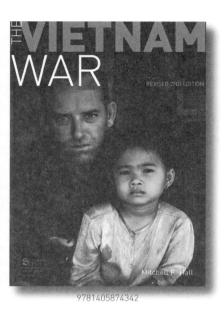

SEMINAR STUDIES
IN HISTORY

9781405874342

9780582771895

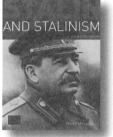

9781405874366

9781405874359

9780582299085

9781405874311

9781405874304

9781405846998

9781405840583

9781405874335

9781405824699

9781405812535

SEMINAR STUDIES

IN HISTORY